The Comedy of Language

THE COMEDY OF LANGUAGE

LANGUAGE

Four Farces by Molière

by Anthony A. Ciccone

 studia humanitatis

Publisher, printer and distributor
José Porrúa Turanzas S. A.
North American Division
1383 Kersey Lane
Potomac, Maryland 20854
U.S.A.

Impreso en Los Estados Unidos
Printed in the United States of America

To my parents

Contents

Part Three: New Directions for Molière Scholarship

Preface

There are essentially two forms of Molière criticism, which Jacques Guicharnaud[1] has designated as "internal" and "external." Internal criticism examines each play according to its place in the evolution of Molière's theater or superposes play upon play within a thematic organization of theatrical, sociological, psychological or philosophical concepts. External studies, on the other hand, seek the dramatist behind the plays, investigating the particular biographical and historical context of their conception. Both forms analyze the language of the plays from important perspectives: external studies examine it stylistically within its historical context, whereas internal studies consider it in its function as the vehicle of ideological positions. And yet, since the use of language implies the entire process by which man seeks to order and give meaning to his world, Molière's particular dramatization of it deserves a more thorough analysis which would apply

---

[1] *Molière: Une Aventure théâtrale* (Paris, 1963), pp. 541–545.

pertinent semiological concepts to an understanding of its structure. The vehicle itself must be studied, both in its use on stage as generator of the comic response and in its global form as indicator of its author's personal theory of communication.

In the first place, since language in Molière's plays seeks to evoke a comic response, the structures of its use in communicative situations between characters must be examined in terms of the laughter they produce. How and why can language itself, in its function as communication, become comic? Only by addressing this transformation can one hope to explain the ultimate purposes of Molière's comedy since in so doing, the critic is forced to investigate how this theater questions the entire phenomenon of normal communicative language, and therefore the process of meaning. Speech which is comic in Molière is only a specific, albeit important, instance of normal communicative language diverted from its usual purposes. It is an example of language's potential to escape a character's control, to express more or less than its speaker intends. When left uncontrolled in this way, language will betray its speaker's true nature when least desired, in the act of communication itself, thereby allowing another to turn this language against him. In Molière's theater, this revealing speech is specifically presented to evoke from the spectator that complex emotional and intellectual reaction whose outward manifestation is laughter. As an instance of man's confrontation with the process of meaning, then, this comic language affords a particular perspective from which to investigate the problematic nature of language itself. Specifically, this language reveals its speaker's being even as this same speaker expresses his perception of the world; it allows a speaker to communicate his desires with the intention of evoking their satisfaction only at the risk of betraying the potential contradiction between these desires and reality.

Secondly, where the unconscious or designed misuse of language is treated systematically by a comic dramatist such as

Molière, one would expect to find an equally systematic, although implicit, judgment of what language's "correct" use should be. Certain critics have sought Molière's sociological or philosophical positions by examining the positions he would ridicule; I would propose that any moral of language presented in his theater could be similarly found in the comparison between this implicit understanding of language and the explicit demonstration of speech-systems which do not respect or control language's normal mechanisms. It is this moral of language, comedy's moral as exemplified by Molière, which I seek to uncover in this study. What role, then, does language play in the internal coherence of each play and in the expression of Molière's particular philosophy of the spoken word?

The transformation of communicative structures into comic language and the implicit theory of language this transformation presupposes can only be fully elaborated in a detailed study of all of Molière's theater, a task which no single work can hope to accomplish. I may in this book, however, open the field to further inquiry by establishing a methodology and applying it to certain plays which seem particularly appropriate. Starting, therefore, with an investigation of language in its communicative function, and using the theoretical structures developed by Saussure, Barthes and Jakobson, I propose a method for examining the limits of language use and the processes by which human language can become comic. In this section, I draw examples from all types of Molière's plays, thus elaborating a general theory. In the second section, I apply this theory to farce, a part of Molière's work which has been too easily overlooked. In this way, I hope to show how a problematic of language use lies at the center of Molière's entire theater, crucial to the analysis of even apparently sketchy farces as well as to the understanding of their author's implied linguistic philosophy. In Part Three, I summarize the methodological consequences of my analysis of farce and indicate possible applications to more extensive plays.

I would like to express my sincere appreciation to Professors T. Jefferson Kline, Gérard Bucher, and John K. Simon for their insights and personal encouragement throughout the evolution of this work, and especially to my typist and most severe critic, my wife Susan.

Part One
METHODOLOGY

I.   Comedy, Comic, Comic of Language

The object of our analysis, language in its function of communication in Molière, depends for its transformation into "comic" language on the generation of a specific relationship between dramatist, characters, and audience. Where this relationship is effected, the general terms "comic theater," "the comic," and "laughter" may be used to designate its observable elements: "comic theater" refers to the nature of the "text" presented; "the comic," to the units of this text, sequences of verbal exchange between characters; "laughter," to the audience response associated with these sequences. Yet we cannot be content to define the comic language solely on this basis, for each of these elements operates within a multiplicity of domains beyond that of the theatrical spectacle of comedy. "Laughter" is not limited to situations involving "comic" language, and such situations are themselves not limited to their manifestation in "comic theater." Furthermore, the notion of "comic theater" is itself a complex one; it may be applied to a vast array of disparate plays from the sketchiest farce to the most developed "comédie de moeurs." To assume, then, that the comic language can be defined simply by what is laughable, or that the comic theater is merely a sequence of laughable verbal exchanges, is to resort to a circular and deceptive reasoning which obscures these concepts and leaves each fundamentally undetermined. What specifically in language evokes laughter in comic theater? How does this laughter represent a particular manifestation of the response we often crudely generalize according to acoustic resemblance? More importantly, what is the relationship between the comic of verbal exchange and the comic in general? Finally, what is the specific role of comic theater in the process which transforms such verbal exchange into the comic? Such questions require that we examine in further depth the nature of comedy, the comic, and laughter, so that we may indicate what specific aspects of these concepts are emphasized by our particular object, language which provokes laughter in Molière's theater. In order to effect this examination, we will foresake the theorist's usual position as spectator for the more objective perspective of observer of the entire interplay of text, verbal exchange, and response. Such a perspective will enable us to develop precise and consistent definitions of comedy, the comic, and laughter for our study of the techniques of language's comic transformation.

In order to understand the comic language created in verbal exchange, we must first define the term "comic." Observing the theatrical spectacle of comedy, we would be inclined to consider laughter as its infallible sign, yet this judgment does not enable us to specify the nature of the object or situation found laughable or the emotion that this response manifests. Closer observation reveals the presence of two successive phenomena similar to those found in any usual stimulus-response situation: one or several characters engage in a conversation of a certain length, the audience reacts by laughing. Not everyone laughs, however, and even among those that do there are observable differences in the timing, duration, and intensity of their laughter. Since we observed

4

the same activity presented to all, however, the variations in the response to this presentation must result from variations in how this activity was evaluated. The immediate cause of laughter, then, cannot be the activity itself, which is purely representational, but rather a particular *interpretation* of it. This interpretation, moreover, is a factor of certain conditions within the spectator himself, not the least of which may be the realization that the activity he observes is merely theatrical and of no immediate, physical consequence to him. The activity presented in theater cannot be defined as comic, therefore, simply because it is followed by laughter. Each spectator observes the same activity, yet if the conditions necessary for the comic interpretation are not generated or acknowledged, either he does not laugh, or laughs for reasons which are not intrinsically related to the activity observed.[2] The effect of this variable nature of laughter on the definition of the comic can be summarized as follows:

(1) The comic is not inherent to a particular activity, but rather is something attributable to any activity when certain conditions are generated *and* acknowledged.

(2) The laughter associated with any activity is actually a response to this activity in its *interpreted* form.

There would be further difficulties in assuming that the comic and laughter are mutually designatory. Although we may presume that wherever the comic is found the result is laughter, the latter is a heterogeneous phenomenon which can express a multitude of emotions. Within theater as well as without, we often observe what seems to be a laughter of pure joy, of relief, of scorn, bewilderment, admiration, all expressed by an identical psycho-physiological response-form; we would find it difficult, however, to declare that the activi-

---

[2] e.g., the ineptness of the actors, the desire to be included in the group of appreciative spectators, etc.

ties which evoke these various emotions are all comic. Either we conclude that both the comic and laughter involve all these emotions, which we do not believe to be the case, or that when we say that the comic evokes laughter, we mean a specific type of laughter associated with a particular emotion. Since types of laughter are difficult to distinguish, however, it seems more appropriate to define the comic according to more objectively observable criteria. We are thus led to a third precision of the comic:

> (3) Although often observed in conjunction with laughter, the activity judged *comic* is at first a neutral structure which seeks to motivate in its interpreted form only one or several of the emotions laughter in general may express.

Let us attempt to define the primary emotion motivated by the comic by examining the interpretative process through which any activity may be judged comic.

Mauron has indicated that the principal aspect of the comic interpretation is the comparison between two representations:

> La première est cette prévision probable de l'instant à venir que nous faisons à chaque minute . . . . [La seconde] est la représentation de l'événement réel.[3]

Laughter within this system is generated by a discrepancy between these representations, yet as such it has no specific object. At the outset, this laughter is a rather mechanical response to an unexpected difference between what we expect to happen and what we observe happening. The notion of comparison, however, implies that one of these representations be judged "inappropriate" in terms of the other. We may thus distinguish between two stages of laughter: a purely mechanical response to difference and a more conscious evaluation of the terms which differ. This conscious laughter

---

[3] Charles Mauron, *Psychocritique du genre comique* (Paris, 1964), pp. 18–19.

6

may have two possible objects, both of which may thus be considered comic: where the spectator judges his own "prévision probable" to have been inappropriate, he becomes himself the object of his laughter; where the observed representation is judged inappropriate, the spectator directs his laughter against one or several of its participants. In both situations, this judgment implies that the spectator feels superior to *someone*, as well as to some particular *action*: in the first case, his past self, and in the second, the character(s) he observes. Although both objects may become comic through such a judgment, we believe that laughter in the spectacle of comic theater is primarily directed against the character observed. Many of Molière's "fourbes" invite admiration and therefore a feeling of inferiority on the part of the spectator, who would at times be forced to admit that he, too, would have been deceived by their machinations. The spectator of comedy, however, is immediately saved from such embarrassment by the very fact that, objectively speaking, this inferiority has no consequences. He is thus in most cases freed to direct his laughter against the characters he observes. Indeed, comedy's principal technique seems to be the inclusion of the spectator within the game of deception as "fourbe" himself, specifically by making him supremely aware of what is to occur and refusing this awareness to any one or all of the characters under observation. Two further aspects of the comic are thus indicated:

(4) The comic results from a feeling of superiority, and thus the comic laughter may have two objects: spectator or character.

(5) In comedy, it is primarily the spectator's superiority to the character(s) observed which is rendered operable.

Let us examine this role of comedy in the creation of the comic by again clearly distinguishing between the two concepts in question.

If the comic involves the comparison between an external, objective activity and an internal, subjective judgment of

7

what this activity should be, we must be dealing with two distinct domains, one purely representational, the other normative. It is the latter which actually determines whether the observed activity is comic, yet as we have shown, it is beyond *direct* stimulation by this activity in its uninterpreted form. It is apparent, however, that certain activities are more likely than others to produce a feeling of superiority in the spectator and therefore be interpreted as comic. What must occur in the presentation of such activities is a certain "conditioning" of the spectator's normative faculty. This faculty, we believe, is the product of two distinguishable movements: the entire socio-psychological history of the individual spectator, both ontogenetic and phylogenetic, and his immediate condition created by the atmosphere of the play he is observing; that is, what he would usually expect and what he has been led to expect in this particular instance. It is only the former which is untouchable in theater, and although it is often crucial to the comic interpretation, its nature can only be taken into account and played upon, but never modified. The immediate condition of the spectator can be influenced, however, and we believe this influence is the key to understanding the process by which a purely descriptive activity evokes a normative, subjective response. If a neutral activity may be interpreted as comic when observed on stage yet not comic when it occurs outside the sphere of theater, the transformation must be due to a variation in context. In our analysis, this deciding context is comedy.[4]

In theater, as in any literary form, the spectator or reader confronts a number of signs composed of a content and an expression and presented linearly. These signs are combined

---

[4] It must be understood that by "comedy" here we are not only referring to comic theater, which is a specific *form* of comedy, but rather to an ensemble of techniques, some of which are reproducible outside of theater as well as within. Common to both domains is the use of "third-person narration," for instance, implicit in theater since the dramatist himself is never implicated on stage, often explicit in comic anecdotes whose subject is usually the foibles of another.

in sequences of varying length which create in their totality the text in question. In our analysis, these sequences of signs, units of verbal exchange between characters, serve as the context within which the use of each sign is to be interpreted and evaluated. Yet these sign-sequences are themselves elements of larger systems of meaning, the work's sociological, philosophical, and psychological discourse. Thus we may distinguish three levels of sign-operation and therefore three levels of analysis:[5]

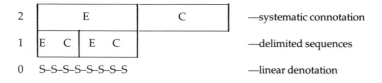

2	E		C	—systematic connotation
1	E C	E C		—delimited sequences
0	S–S–S–S–S–S–S–S			—linear denotation

As a sequence of delimited units of meaning, an instance of verbal exchange reveals a particular relationship between the signs which comprise it and the meaning attributed to these signs by the interlocutors involved. This attribution, whether conscious or unconscious, serves as the basis for specific systems of additional meanings or "sens seconds." Such sequences therefore require a double effort of decoding on the part of the analyst: in the first case, he must determine the nature of the relationship between sign and meaning for each interlocutor; in the second case, the implications this relationship may have within the context of the entire play:

2	encoding/decoding process demonstrated		implicit meaning(s) of this process	2nd decoding
1	sign	meaning attributed to this sign		1st decoding

---

[5] The diagrams and working definitions used to the end of this paragraph are based on Roland Barthes' discussion of denotation and connotation in *Eléments de sémiologie* (Paris, 1964), pp. 163–168. They have been adapted here for the purpose of explaining the structure of specifically theatrical language.

Such an interpretation reveals two types of comparison possible between spectator and character: the meaning each attributes to the specific signs in question (contextual competence) on one hand, and their respective awareness of the consequences of the attributory process implied (connotative competence) on the other.

As a specific type of theatrical text, comedy offers its spectator a particular demonstration of the sign's contextual and connotative references. The signs used in verbal exchange are never comic of themselves, since they are neutral in their denotative meanings as are all signs. They become potentially comic, however, once their contextual inappropriateness is revealed through their inadequate use. The perception of this inappropriateness by the spectator most often results from a superior decoding of the connotative implications of such exchanges. The "comic" then, is actually a judgment whose existence depends on a certain "reading" of the sign by the spectator which differs from its explicit or implicit "reading" on stage. "Comedy" in this perspective can be considered the global context of these sequences of inappropriately used signs which allows such inappropriateness to be interpreted specifically as comic. In our analysis of the heterogeneity of laughter, we identified the locus of this interpretation as a particular psychological state of the spectator. Comedy, it seems, consists primarily of those techniques which seek to create in this spectator the necessary conditions for such a state to exist. It is the rhetorical system which invites the spectator to "read" a certain sequence of verbal units as more than simple narrative signs and to compare this reading to its theatrical counterparts with the specific purpose of judging his reading justifiably superior. Let us examine several of this system's principal techniques and indicate how they are realized by the comic language.

We have seen that the principal condition of the comic interpretation is the superior decoding ability of the spectator.

Such superiority is merely the basis for irony, however, and not all irony is comic. Indeed, a certain superiority seems inherent to the role of the spectator itself, for he alone witnesses, and therefore *may* comprehend the connotative meanings of, all verbal exchanges which occur on stage. Where only this "positional" superiority is operable, however, there can be no "comic" as we understand the term. Even where it may give rise to laughter, this laughter may exist in comedy, tragedy, farce, or "drame," and as such, is not a viable criterion for distinguishing between these theatrical forms. We believe, however, that comedy seeks to exploit this inherent "positional" superiority in a precise way by *justifying* it; its surest technique is the demonstration of inferiority as an avoidable yet understandably logical consequence of character misperception or misinterpretation. This "justifiable" superiority does not therefore depend on the inherent theatrical distance between character and spectator, but rather on the latter's action of *taking distance* from the former. Let us examine this notion in further detail.

Numerous theories of comedy insist on the separation between spectator and character as a necessary condition for the comic judgment. Yet where total and continual separation exists, the comic is impossible since no terms for comparison are present. The comic character cannot be totally foreign to the spectator, therefore, and any perception or interpretation of reality he may demonstrate, however eccentric, must be, in Bergson's terms, "human."[6] Although comedy presupposes this similarity, its principal purpose is differentiation; from the totality of possible human behaviors, the comic dramatist chooses to emphasize and demonstrate those which he believes are, or should be considered, in some way aberrant. These behaviors are not presented in a vacuum, however,

---

[6] Henri Bergson, *Le Rire: Essai sur la signification du comique* (Paris, 1972), p. 2.

since they are compared and contrasted *on stage* to "normal" behavior. The process of differentiation, therefore, is inherent to the comic text itself for this text presents both terms necessary for comparison. The separation between spectator and comic character is thus effected objectively by the very movement of comedy: presenting the comic character only insofar as he differs initially from others of his own world, yet ultimately from the spectator as well.

Comedy does not merely demonstrate difference, although this may be its most basic technique. Comedy specifically presents those differences which indicate ridiculousness and inferiority. Two interdependent techniques seem to operate to this purpose, either or both of which may be employed in any given play: on one hand, a character may himself betray unwittingly the logical insufficiency of his perception of reality; on the other, such insufficiency may be demonstrated by other characters who manipulate it in such a way as to deny any possible behavioral effectiveness. The result in both instances is similar: the comic character finds himself in an isolation either unwittingly chosen or as the demonstrated logical consequence of his behavior. Not only is this behavior revealed as ineffective, but such ineffectiveness becomes in the more tightly structured comedies the very reason for the effectiveness of the other's behavior. Thus in *Le Bourgeois Gentilhomme*, for example, it is supremely appropriate that Jourdain fall prey to the trappings of the nobility he unconsciously sought in exactly this form.

When we accept, therefore, the theory that the comic interpretation is primarily an intellectual judgment which requires a certain silencing of our affective sympathy, we are not referring to an arbitrary decision. The spectator does not arbitrarily withhold his sympathy from the comic character, but rather this character invites such restraint by his own actions. This is perhaps comedy's most important purpose and it is intimately related to its movement of differentiation.

Any play at least begins with characters who have an equal claim to our sympathy; we attribute to each, moreover, a certain minimal behavioral efficiency and morality. The comic character, however, is forever demonstrating himself inferior to these standards and thus inviting our ridicule. Our particular analysis will focus on a specific area of human behavior which is involved in this demonstration of inferiority—man's ability to use language for effective communication. We believe that by investigating this particularly crucial domain of the human situation we may uncover several important clues to the nature and purpose of comic language for Molière in particular and for comedy itself in general. Before we can determine what constitutes inadequate linguistic behavior, however, we must first examine the nature of man's relationship to language and the limitations already inherent to language's use in communication.

II. Man versus Language: Powers and Limitations

Since our analysis will seek the comic wherever language escapes the control of its speaker in the act of communication, we must determine to what extent this escape is inherent to language itself. If it were the *nature* of language to be totally beyond man's effective use, it would be difficult to imagine how its escape from man could become comic in any particular *instance* of its inadequate use. To argue simply that the comic in language exists because there are instances of language's communicative use which evoke laughter would be to beg the question, since it would substitute one undetermined notion for another. The general relationship of the speaking subject to language itself must be our first concern, if we are to understand the potential of this relationship to become comic as we have defined this term.

The human condition finds its clearest expression in man's continuing struggle to make sense of the world and communicate this sense to others. His necessary recourse to language for the satisfaction of this desire risks to betray him, however, in the very appropriation of language's systems. While permitting the generalization and communicability of a "prise de conscience" of the world and a relationship to it, this personal appropriation creates a definition of the speaker who formulates it which can never be transcended. Roland Barthes has seen the foundation of a fundamentally tragic relationship between man and language in this inability to be anything other than what speech would designate:

> . . . chaque homme est prisonnier de son langage: hors de sa classe, le premier mot le signale, le situe entièrement et l'affiche avec toute son histoire. L'homme est offert, livré par son langage, trahi par une vérité formelle qui échappe à ses mensonges intéressés ou généreux. *La diversité des langages fonctionne donc comme une Nécessité, et c'est pour cela qu'elle fonde un tragique.*[7]

According to Barthes, man is forever condemned to the limits of his own speech; he can never be other than a language which has been determined in advance by inescapable historical, sociological and psychological influences. Implicit, then, in every instance of "il dit" is an "il est," a message of essence which exposes its speaker as a definable sociological and psychological product.[8]

If in expressing himself, man actually encodes two messages simultaneously, one of which can define him, he risks no less a definition by the responses which indicate his understanding of another's expression. For in the process of decoding, any instance of "il comprend" implies an "il est"

---

[7] Roland Barthes, *Le Degré zéro de l'écriture* (Paris: 1964), p. 70.

[8] The use of third person pronouns here is not gratuitous, for the power of language to designate its speaker implies a listener who is sensitive to this designation. The "il dit" and "il est" forms of these messages serve to indicate this transformation of speech into observable symptoms. The same notion will be the basis for our use of "il comprend" in our analysis of designation by decoding.

similar to that revealed in the process of encoding. G.A. Miller has clarified this idea in his discussion of Saussure's "circuit de la parole,"[9] which postulated a passivity in decoding:

> Percevoir le discours n'est pas chose passive et automatique. Celui qui perçoit assume une fonction sélective en répondant à certains aspects de la situation globale et non à d'autres. *Il répond aux stimuli selon une organisation qu'il leur impose.* Et il remplace la stimulation absente ou contradictoire d'une manière compatible avec ses besoins et son expérience passée.[10]

Although Miller seems to emphasize the role of local (i.e. situational) influences on decoding, it is evident that these influences are rooted in the same types of systems Barthes has implied. The connection lies in the term "expérience passée," since this is obviously a factor of the decoder's historical, sociological and psychological situation.

We can summarize the double message inherent to any encoding and decoding of language as follows:

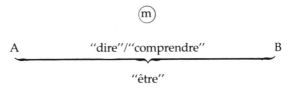

where A = speaker, B = listener, m = the message encoded or decoded, and M = the nature of the speaker implicitly communicated by the encoding or decoding process (either consciously or unconsciously). The celebrated Cartesian

[9] Ferdinand de Saussure, *Cours de linguistique générale* (Paris, 1972), pp. 28–29.

[10] George A. Miller, *Langage et Communication* (Paris, 1956), p. 111.

implication, "Je pense donc je suis," must therefore be rewritten:

Il dit/comprend X comme A, donc il est A.

Condemned to speak, therefore, yet incapable of transcending his speech, man's position vis-à-vis language seems indeed a restricted one. To the degree that he is automatically and irrevocably a prisoner of his language, insofar as in both his encoding and decoding (m) this language can reveal him for what he is (M) and restrict him to this designation, then his situation is potentially tragic.

It follows, however, that this power of language to define its encoder or decoder is actually the necessary condition if man is to have any definition whatsoever. If a speaker is immediately defined once he speaks, it follows that he remains *undefined* until he does so. Creation and restriction of designation are actually one process, then, and are mutually implicative: any definition is created only because it is restrictive and vice versa. Once this fact is accepted, we can understand how language's designatory power can be controlled by man. In fact, man can even exploit this power in order to allow the creation of a *certain* designation where it would serve his purposes. Man may indeed have no control over the designation created by his use of language in communication once his message has been articulated. He has, however, a significant *potential* control over what he chooses to say and consequently over what he becomes by saying it. This control results from an acquired *awareness* of language's power to designate his being. Thus, for example, if I wished to present myself as a native French speaker to an audience which understood no French whatsoever, I would need only to pronounce some sounds vaguely reminiscent of this language to be accepted as such. If I wished to continue this for audiences with a greater knowledge of French, I would be required to formulate my expressions more carefully. If I unwittingly attempted the same trick before an actual French audience, however, I would be im-

17

mediately exposed. This example reveals that if the designating message "il est" is a function of my choice of "je dis," then to the degree that I can control the choice of "je dis," I control the creation of the particular restrictive "il est" message which results. An important corollary to this fact, which we will investigate subsequently in further detail, is that language's designation of a speaker is a function of a *listener* who must be capable of distinguishing between deceptive and actual designation. Just as a speaker can create a designation (M) only by a convincing encoding of his message (m), so also a listener can see through this designation only by a decoding roughly equal or superior to the encoding he observes.

Where an interlocutor is aware of language's designatory power, the potentially tragic formulation of his relationship to language must be revised:

je dis/comprends X comme A, donc *je* suis A

or, to include the consecutive roles of speaker (D_1) and listener (D_2):

Si je disais/comprenais X comme A, je *serais* A pour D_1 / D_2

The shift to the conditional implies a choice in coding, evidenced by, for example, the time-lag involved between the encoding/decoding of the message in question and the designation subsequently created.

We can thus summarize the principal points of our analysis of man's relationship to language as follows:

(1) Language always involves *two* messages, a "dire"/"comprendre" and an "être."

(2) The instance of "dire"/"comprendre" reveals the nature of "être."

(3) Therefore, every use of language automatically defines this user.

(4) However, since "dire"/"comprendre" implies "être," to the degree that man chooses the former, he controls the latter.

18

(5) Therefore, if language can define man, man can choose his definition.

In short, then, the power of language to designate man *need not be* beyond his control. Our analysis has revealed that man can become aware of this power and can, through this awareness, escape its determinism.[11] This potential awareness, insofar as it places the process of self-determination within man's grasp, creates for him the possibility of either grandeur or ridicule. These possibilities can only exist within a system that admits of the freedom to choose. Since man is normally capable of attaining such an awareness, and using it to guarantee his recognition in the particular role he may choose, we would consider any man who does not demonstrate this awareness as ridiculous. This judgment may be justifiable or not, as we shall examine subsequently, for demonstration is always demonstration for someone. The inability or refusal to recognize such a demonstration can be as damning a comic judgment of a listener as of a speaker.

Man's control of language's revelatory power would be simple to exploit were it not for the existence of two other fundamental necessities of communication, the code and the listener. In the first place, the believability of a speaker's chosen designation depends, as we have briefly indicated, on the convincing *formulation* of the particular messages (m) which would create such a designation (M). Secondly, no matter how skillful this formulation may be, its ultimate effectiveness always depends on the capacities and predispositions

---

[11] Usage reveals that man demonstrates this awareness even when he is not completely conscious of the control it affords him. For example, "Speaking strictly as an economist. . . ," or "If I were to consider this as a psychologist, I would say. . . ."

19

of its listener or decoder. Is man's control of language's designatory power merely an illusion, then, since the formulation of his choices is governed by the constraints inherent to the code chosen (for our purposes, linguistic) and by a reliance on the arbitrary decoding of an unpredictable listener? Is man in the ironic position of being able to choose his role only to have it escape him in its formulation and reception?

The problem of arbitrary decoding by an unpredictable listener must be investigated along two interdependent lines: To what degree is decoding arbitrary? To what degree is the listener unpredictable? In order to answer these two questions, we must realize that the observed response to any stimulus is *not* normally the decoded product but rather is the *result of* the contact between the original stimulus decoded *and* a second stimulus from the decoder himself. We can outline this as follows:

$$S'T \longrightarrow S'R \longrightarrow S'D \dashrightarrow \overset{\displaystyle RS'D \relbar\joinrel\relbar S2}{} \dashrightarrow RST$$

$$\vdash\joinrel\relbar \text{ unobservable } \relbar\joinrel\dashv$$

where $S'T$ = the original stimulus in its transmitted form, $S'R$ = this stimulus in its received form, $S'D$ = this stimulus in its decoded form, $RS'D$ = the response to this stimulus in the listener, $S2$ = a second stimulus not necessarily related to the original, and RST = the response which we observe which is actually the product of $RS'D$ and $S2$. For example, given S' = /2 + 2 = ?/ and RST = "Four," then

$$S'T = \text{"What are } 2 + 2?\text{"}$$
$$S'R = \text{"What are } 2 + 2?\text{"}$$
$$S'D = /2,2,+,?/$$
$$RS'D = \text{compliance/non-compliance + comprehension/}$$
$$\text{non-comprehension}$$
$$S2 = 2 + 2 = 4$$
$$RST = \text{"Four."}$$

Note that the correct answer depends in this case specifically on a positive reaction to the question, compliance, as well as an understanding of the concepts involved, comprehension. If *either* element is lacking, RST could become "Five" or "Do it yourself"; if *both* are lacking, "What do you mean, what are 2 + 2?" or something akin to it. Once this process is understood and we no longer confuse the response observed (RST) with the stimulus decoded (S'D), we can recognize that RST is actually the result of a decoding *plus encoding* process. If this is the case, then the choice of a particular response is potentially just as arbitrary as the choice of a particular stimulus; the response is a function of more than simply the original stimulus in question, and therefore its motivation is just as undiscoverable. If this remained true, no communication could ever be assured. Since the latter is contrary to observed facts, we must assume that the response we observe (RS'T) must undergo several modifications, all of which can be influenced by a given speaker.[12] Our point is simply this: the arbitrariness of the decoding process can be reduced by making the second stimulus (S2) correspond as closely as possible to the logic of the original stimulus transmitted (S'T). We will examine subsequently the processes by which such a correspondence can be obtained, but for the moment will simply conclude that such a correspondence is obtainable.

The response effected by a speaker through the transmission of a particular stimulus is, as we have demonstrated, the result of encoding as well as decoding. To the degree that this speaker can control the second stimulus which motivates

---

[12] cf. Jakobson's analysis of idiolect in "Deux aspects de langage et deux types d'aphasie," reprinted in *Essais de linguistique générale*, (Paris, 1963):

"En parlant à un nouvel interlocuteur, chacun essaye toujours, *délibérément ou involontairement*, de se découvrir un vocabulaire commun: soit pour plaire, soit simplement pour se faire comprendre, soit enfin pour se débarrasser de lui, on emploie les termes du destinataire." (p. 54)

this encoding, he can control the response desired. As we have demonstrated earlier, the process of encoding creates a double message, (m) and (M), the latter serving to designate the nature of the speaker. If this is the case, responses of the type we have been considering must reveal certain patterns of association or behavior in their creators. These patterns are the keys to reducing the unpredictability of the listener. By articulating certain similar responses, the listener (or respondent) increases the predictability of his behavior. If it is true that no human being is ever completely predictable, it is just as true that all are predictable to a certain degree. This predictability, moreover, can be increased with the observation of their linguistic performances. To take up our original example, suppose I presented the following series of questions and obtained the answers which correspond below:

$$S: \quad 3 + 3 = ?$$
$$R: \quad 6$$

$$S: \quad 4 + 4 = ?$$
$$R: \quad 8$$

etc.

I could then reasonably assume that a response of "Five" to 2 + 2 = ?" was motivated by a desire not to comply and *not* because of difficulty in comprehension. I could then work directly on gaining such compliance, having isolated the particular decoding obstacle involved. [13]

No listener is completely unpredictable, therefore, since society furnishes all of us with general labels, producer or consumer, man or woman, liberal or conservative, which betray our predispositions to anyone who is aware of them. In

---

[13] Our example of course precludes any physical or neurological difficulties in the respondent.

short, then, any decoder is presumably known to a certain degree even before he responds. To the degree he allows such labels to dictate his responses, however, he assures the exposure of such predispositions to an encoder who would use this knowledge to manipulate him. By careful observation of the patterns of such decoding, any encoder can become capable of predicting a particular response to any stimulus he might propose, and thus in this sense, remove the obstacle of decoder unpredictability where it suits his purposes.[14]

Although any response which is the result of the decoding process is potentially as arbitrary as any encoded stimulus, our analysis of decoding has demonstrated that the chances of evoking a particular desired response can be increased. This control of the decoder would be impossible, however, without the potential to manipulate the linguistic signs which are used in the formulation of the stimulus-message (m) destined to effect a response appreciative of the desired designation. Yet these signs function only within an already elaborated system ("langue") which codifies them in certain patterns and controls their linear combination according to certain regulatory laws. Does this anterior codification of meaningful signs remove the process of meaning from man's control and thus limit its purposeful use? This apparently paradoxical situation, wherein on one hand, language limits the meaning of its signs and on the other, man modifies the

---

[14] Implicit in our analysis to this point has been the identification between guaranteeing a particular response (faire faire) and creating a particular role (se faire reconnaître). The two activities derive from the same technique of control of language's revelatory power by the convincing formulation of messages (m) within normal verbal exchange, although there are instances where one may take precedence over the other. Scapin, for instance, deals mainly with control of responses, whereas Tartuffe relies more extensively on the creation of a role.

meaning of these same signs, can only be resolved by examining language's systematic functioning.

How does language ("langue") create meaning? Saussure has indicated that the principal role of "langue" is one of delimitation:

> Le rôle caractéristique de la langue vis-à-vis de la pensée [est] de servir d'intermédiaire entre la pensée et le son, *dans des conditions telles que leur union aboutit nécessairement à des délimitations réciproques d'unités.*[15]

The "unités" which result from this delimitation cannot be said to be meaningful, however, until they are considered in their relationship to one another. Thus, Saussure's distinction between "signification" and "valeur": the former is determined by the relationship between concept and linguistic sign, the latter by the relationship between linguistic signs themselves within the system.[16] The function of "langue" as system, then, is to create signs which are purely differential, that is, signs which cannot be said to possess meaning of themselves, but rather only by virtue of their capacity to allow differentiation between concepts and between other signs. The system by which the meaning of a sign is created, then, is identical to the system by which this meaning is limited, for without the delimiting of thought and sound into "unités" and the delimiting of "unités" into signs, no meaning would be possible: "Ce qui distingue un signe, voilà tout ce qui le constitue."[17] If the linguistic sign is pure differentiation, then the system which created it also determines it. If all signs were subject to the whims of every individual speaker both for their creation and combination, that is, if there were no such reality as a "système-langue," then no sign would be meaningful.

---

[15] Saussure, *C.L.G.*, p. 156.
[16] Saussure, *C.L.G.*, p. 160.
[17] Saussure, *C.L.G.*, p. 168.

The same system that limits the meaning of a sign is the sole reason this sign has any meaning whatsoever.

Wherein, then, lies man's potential to affect these signs? If language's ("langue") function as system is to create meaningful signs by delimitation and order their combination according to certain rules, these signs exist only virtually within this system. "Langue," in this sense, can be compared to *code*, a structure of meaningful elements created and ordered with the purpose of guaranteeing mutual comprehension:

> [La langue est] un *trésor* déposé par la pratique de la parole dans les sujets appartenant à une même communauté, un *système* grammatical existant *virtuellement* dans chaque cerveau, ou plus exactement dans les cerveaux d'un ensemble d'individus . . . Elle est l'ensemble des habitudes linguistiques qui permettent à un sujet de comprendre et de se faire comprendre.[18]

This system, however, depends for its realization on the individual act of speech, an act which presupposes this code yet in and by which these codified elements are selected and combined in infinite variation and complexity. As selection, "la parole" depends totally on the already codified entities of "la langue": the speaker is free to choose only from the particular stock of phonemes, lexemes, and syntactic structures which his language has selected and combined. As combination, however, "la parole" functions with increasing freedom, since the sentence can be considered the most complex structure governed by the "système-langue." As Jakobson has indicated, the code permits no freedom in the creation of phonemes and very little in the combination of phonemes into words. However:

> Dans la formation des phrases à partir des mots, la contrainte que subit le locuteur est moindre. Enfin, dans la combinaison des

---

[18] Saussure, *C.L.G.*, pp. 30, 112.

phrases en énoncés, l'action des règles contraignantes de la syntaxe s'arrête et la liberté de tout locuteur particulier s'accroît substantiellement . . .[19]

The sentence, and its extension in "discours," then, are formulated in an atmosphere of limited freedom. This freedom lies at the center of the process of meaning since, as we have indicated earlier, no sign can be said to be meaningful until its relationship to other signs has been determined. The function of "la parole" can thus be considered as the creation of a *context* for the particular signs its speaker selects, as the specification of their meaning. This ability to create context, then, places the control of meaning within man's reach. In this sense, "la parole" brings into play a specific set of meanings which are, on one hand, *social*, in that they imply a common code, yet on the other hand, *individual*, since they result from particular operation(s) on the relationship between the signs which constitute these meanings.

Whereas "langage" involves the simultaneous messages "dire" (m) and "être" (M), therefore, the act of speech reveals that this "m" is actually double as well, implicating both the speaker's use of the code and the particular contextual modifications resulting from the combinations of its elements. The two interdependent "sub-messages" will furnish us with two of our more important categories for evaluating the linguistic behavior of any speaker: competence (m^1), the phonetic, syntactic, and semantic adequacy of a speaker's utterances, and performance (m^2), the appropriateness and communicability of the contextual modifications of meaning created by these utterances. Since Jakobson's pertinent investigation of abnormal speech, these contextual modifications have become the center of interest for numerous disciplines, for their two principal forms, metaphor and metonymy, have been seen to

---

[19] Jakobson, p. 47.

correspond to the two principal categories of human perception, similarity/difference and contiguity/non-contiguity. We will pursue this connection further in subsequent sections, for the moment simply concluding from our analysis that these modifications, while founded on the structures of "langue," find their ultimate significance in the individual act of "parole."

We began our analysis with the hypothesis that we would seek the comic in language wherever we encountered language diverted from its "normal" uses, either unconsciously or designedly. This hypothesis, we discovered, although certainly indicating a necessary condition for the comic, proved to be too broad. There are definitely instances of language's designed misuse which are, if not tragic, at least serious. Political rhetoric, for example, which often exploits irrational fear, could scarcely be considered comic despite the fact that it is perhaps the most striking system of designedly misused language. Nor is unconsciously misused language any more automatically comic. A child's speech is egocentric because he has no idea that language should be used to communicate; an aphasic, while perhaps recognizing this function, is physically or psychologically incapable of modifying his speech to render this function operable. The simple misuse of language, then, is insufficient by itself to produce the comic.

In order to tighten our original hypothesis, we proposed subsequently an investigation of the intrinsic limits of man's relationship to language itself. This investigation revealed that on all levels, language imposed certain controls, to which all men are subject yet within which, *and only by which*, each is allowed at least a marginal latitude. Where "langage" would escape man by threatening to reveal his particular historical and psychological being, thereby exposing his nature in the very act of communicating his desires, we showed that the potential awareness of this power placed its control within man's reach. Where this awareness would have seemed useless in the face of an unpredictable listener, we showed that this listener's linguistic behavior could become predictable enough to allow his possible control. Where this predictability would have seemed impossible to exploit, given the already codified meaning of the signs destined to assure the desired response, we showed that these signs depended ultimately for their meaning on their combination according to the wishes of their user. The possibility of circumventing language's designatory power, the potential to control speech in its three major aspects of encoding, transmission, and decoding—these were the abilities we found within man's reach.

Again, however, the non-realization of these potential abilities proved necessary but not sufficient for language to become comic. Although assuring us that man could control his linguistic behavior, thereby disproving the theory that the comic was merely a reaction to man's presumed a priori absurd position within an already determined system, the existence of these potential abilities did nothing to explain how some men realize them whereas others do not. How, for instance, do some men succeed in convincing others of the validity of their discourse, thereby acquiring the potential to manipulate them? More importantly, how and why should such manipulation and, where it fails, self-betrayal, be considered comic? In order to answer these questions and further define the nature of the comic language created in this particular use of speech for the expression of desire, we must investigate the workings of the communicative act itself.

III. Theatrical Structures of Communication and the Comic

Let us examine language as it is used in normal communication between two speakers. All that is *directly* observable to the non-participant is a deceptively simple situation: the first interlocutor (D_1) makes a statement (X); the second interlocutor (D_2) responds in word or action (Y). Assuming that D_1 responds verbally, we observe only statement X and statement Y, or in behaviorist terminology, a stimulus (S) and a response (R). Yet both the statement-stimulus and the statement-response are products of anterior operations, the encoding of X' and Y', or more specifically

$$\text{encoding of } X' = \frac{\text{sequence of signifiants} \quad (X)}{\text{sequence of signifiés} \quad (X)'}$$

$$\text{encoding of } Y' = \frac{\text{sequence of signifiants} \quad (Y)}{\text{sequence of signifiés} \quad (Y)'}$$

where X, Y are the result of phonetic, lexicological, and syntactic choices and X', Y', the result of corresponding semantic choices.

In addition to these primarily linguistic operations, we may assume that the following psychological ones have already taken place, although they may not necessarily be conscious or exact:

(1) Statement X is the response to the perception and conceptualization of a "lack" (interior/exterior).

(2) This "lack" has been encoded psychologically; that is, it has undergone linguistic modifications which seek to formulate it, communicate it, and effect its satisfaction.

The formulation of statement Y is fundamentally similar yet perhaps more complicated, since the decoded product on which it depends is not usually directly observable:

(3) Statement Y is the response to the communication of a "lack" as decoded (RS'D).

(4) This response has been encoded psychologically; that is, it has undergone linguistic modifications which seek to indicate comprehension, communicate this comprehension, and agree/refuse to satisfy the "lack" communicated.

Including Saussure's notions of "phonation" and "audition," we may thus outline the typical verbal exchange as shown in the diagram on page 31.

It should be evident from this analysis that the greater part of any instance of communication is potentially (and more often than not, actually) implicit. Although we could imagine a conversation wherein each phase would be explicitly announced, only the encoded stimulus and response are usually heard. Since this is the case, the spoken message itself must bear the burden of assuring the particular desired response.

Considering the statement-stimulus as the linguistically modified response to an interiorized lack enables us to formalize three general purposes of verbal communication of particular interest for our study of communication in comic theater. In the first place, the speaking subject communicates in order to transmit a certain amount of information about his particular physical and/or psychological situation. Secondly,

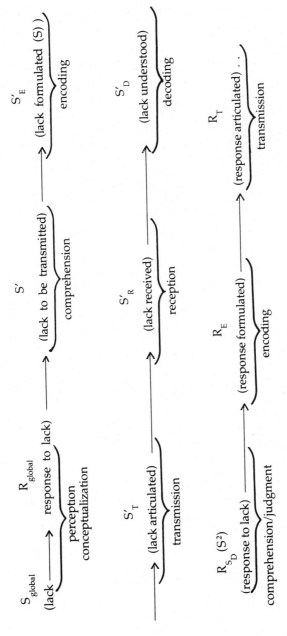

31

this expression concerns more than the simple transference of denotative information, for in formulating it, the speaker himself seeks to become conscious of his subjective position vis-à-vis this situation. Merleau-Ponty has indicated the relationship between these two purposes:

> Exprimer, pour le sujet parlant, c'est prendre conscience; il n'exprime pas seulement pour les autres, il exprime pour savoir lui-même ce qu'il vise. Si la parole veut incarner une *intention significative* qui n'est qu'un certain vide, ce n'est pas seulement pour recréer en autrui le même manque, la même privation, mais encore pour savoir de quoi il y a manque et privation. [20]

Thirdly, the speaking subject often does more than simply communicate the content of his needs; he frames them in such a way as to evoke a response which is adequate for their satisfaction. The addition of this factor, the desire to exploit language's potential persuasive power, completes what we believe to be the primary purposes of communication investigated in comic theater: the speaking subject expresses himself

(a) to become conscious of his position vis-à-vis internal and external needs;

(b) to communicate the objective, factual content of these needs;

(c) to harmonize his listener's response with the satisfaction of these needs.

The delimitation of these purposes furnishes us with three interdependent areas of investigation necessarily involved in the determination of the adequacy of any particular statement: to what degree

(a) does this statement enable its speaker to become conscious of his needs?
(subjective adequacy)

(b) is this statement appropriately formulated to communicate the content of these needs?
(communicability)

---

[20] Maurice Merleau-Ponty, *Signes* (Paris, 1960), p. 113.

(c) is this statement (assuming its communicability) effective in provoking a response which would satisfy these needs? (objective efficacity)

Let us examine each of these purposes in their normal functioning in order to outline a theory of the comic language based on violations of this norm.

Any verbal exchange depends, of course, on the presence of at least two interlocutors and a shared conventional code. It is evident, however, that these three elements in no way guarantee the listener's comprehension nor the efficacity of the speaker's particular statement-stimulus. Indeed, the presence of these three elements cannot guarantee even the physical exchange of statements, for all communication is subject *a priori* to the requirement of successivity. In any instance of verbal exchange, the statement-stimulus and the statement-response must follow each other *chronologically* and cannot occupy the same acoustic time-space. In everyday reality, any two messages simultaneously transmitted reduce each other to zero by their interference. Comic theater, however, differs significantly from this reality in that *every* communicative situation is presented to a spectator for evaluation. In the specific case of simultaneously transmitted statements, as in all cases of theatrical communication, both statements *and the fact of their coincidence* become, in effect, messages for this spectator.[21] We can diagram this situation as follows:

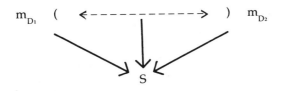

[21] We are assuming here that the theatrical presentation of simultaneously transmitted messages can effect the audition of each message by the spectator. In *Le Mariage forcé*, this is accomplished by presenting messages which begin at the same moment yet vary in length.

The most obvious message presented is the message of coincidence, which reveals immediately D_1's inability to affect D_2 (assuming D_1 is the would-be initiator of any dialogue) as well as D_2's lack of regard for the requirement of successivity. It seems evident that this coincidence would be capable by itself of triggering a comic reaction, for the spectator is in an automatically superior position: he is the sole recipient of *any* message.

In the following analysis, we will deal with the two principal types of messages received by the spectator by the presentation of simultaneously emitted statements. On one hand, both speakers could simply be attempting to contact each other, or to dispute the position of primary speaker. In these instances, the content of their statements is never considered, for this content is merely reduced to "noise" by the interference.[22] On the other hand, in situations where D_1 attempts to contact D_2 while the latter speaks on some completely different topic, the speech of D_2 is directed instead solely to the spectator. In this case, not only is D_2's inadequate notion of communication revealed, but the content of whatever he says is presented for evaluation and judgment as well. This content may or may not be correctly formulated. Where it is, as is the case with Pancrace in *Le Mariage forcé*, the comic judgment bears directly on the non-successivity of its presentation. Where it is not, as is the case with the doctor in *La Jalousie du Barbouillé*, the comic judgment bears on its incongruity as well as on the fact of its non-successivity. We will develop the various nuances of this comic situation in our analysis of farce, for it seems that such a fundamental communicative error will be most likely exploited in plays where few messages ever seem to reach their supposed listener.

---

[22] This is especially true in certain farces, often indicated by the curious lack of continuity in the text itself. Once such interference begins, the reader will often notice a simple "etc., etc." in the place of dialogue. cf. *La Jalousie du Barbouillé*, sc. vi.

The non-coincidence of statements in verbal exchange is not, of course, sufficient to effect communication. Even if we considered this term in its most general definition as the transmission and reception of at least two meaningful statements, even transmission and reception would be impossible if three further requirements were not met: contact between D_1 and D_2 must be assured; D_2 must be given a certain quantity of factual information; and both D_1 and D_2 must share the same comprehension of the message's meaningful units. Jakobson has baptized the linguistic expressions which seek to ensure these necessary elements as language's phatic, referential and metalinguistic functions, respectively.[23] For example, in the statement-stimulus

> Je n'aime pas, vous m'écoutez, qu'on nous espionne, qu'on nous regarde.

the actual message, "Allons nous entretenir en secret," even if only implicit, would never be correctly (or incorrectly) received: (a) if the physical contact between D_1 and D_2 were not guaranteed ("fonction phatique" expressed by "vous m'écoutez"); (b) if the topic or theme of the message were not perceived ("fonction référentielle" expressed by "on nous espionne"); (c) if D_2 did not understand the word "espionne" ("fonction métalinguistique" expressed by the synonymic addition "on nous regarde"). Where fulfilled, these functions guarantee the *communicability* of the message, although they in no way guarantee that this message will generate the response desired by its speaker.

Let us investigate these three functions of communication as a group, leaving aside for the moment those functions which bear on the speaker (emotive), on the listener (conative), and on the message itself (poetic).[24] It is evident from

---

[23] Roman Jakobson, "Linguistique et poétique," in *Essais*, pp. 209 ff.

[24] Our purpose here in separating Jakobson's six functions in this way is not to imply a greater importance for some, for the act of *(continued on page 36)*

our analysis that the phatic, referential, and metalinguistic functions may be explicitly or implicitly operative in the actual verbal exchange. Their use or non-use may often imply a judgment by the speaker of their necessity. In the example cited above, "vous m'écoutez" may imply that the speaker feels the obligation to assure himself of his listener's attention; "qu'on nous espionne," that he may believe his listener is unaware that they are being overheard; "qu'on nous regarde," that he may be unsure of his listener's ability to decode the word "espionne." Where no such explicit expressions were used, we would conclude that the speaker felt none were necessary, that is, that he believed his listener was attentive, aware of the referential context, and (at least) his equal in linguistic competence. It is apparent, moreover, that wherever these assessments are incorrect, no message, no matter how well formulated or articulated, can ever affect its desired respondent.

The phatic function concerns directly the existence of an "acoustic canal" between two interlocutors. The situation of coinciding statements is perhaps the most fundamental violation of this necessity, for this situation reveals a total disregard for the reception of any transmitted message by a listener. Instances of interruption and non-sequitur could be considered violations of this necessity by the respondent, who reveals by such behavior that he has heard none, or only part of, the statement-stimulus. We must examine the psychological reasons for such reactions in their particular theatrical contexts, since not only is the *fact* of partial "hearing" significant, but the *content* of this partiality is often the sign of certain character preoccupations which reveal a perceptual hierarchization. In similar fashion, the assumed satisfaction of the

_____

(continued from page 35) communication requires the co-presence of all, but rather to preview the analysis of different types of plays. Our analysis of farce, for example, will indicate the preponderance of communicative situations transformed into the comic almost entirely through phatic, referential, and metalinguistic inadequacies.

phatic function by a speaker implies a certain attitude toward his message—that it merits of itself to be heard—and toward his listener—that the listener is automatically interested in this message. Such assumptions are not always correct, and in making them without regard to their appropriateness, a speaker can condemn his message to non-reception from the outset.

We would insist on the fact that such violations of the phatic function are not necessarily comic, yet insofar as they are unintentional, they can reveal discrepancies and inadequacies within the cognitive structure of an interlocutor. Since the spectator alone is aware of this, his feeling of decoding superiority is justified. The situation is different, however, where such violations are intentional. Repeated demand for stimulus repetition is one method of assuring a break-down of stimulus-transmission, for it destroys the development of the statement. Repeated insistence on listener "hearing" by the speaker can often create the impression that a logical message is being transmitted when, in fact, none exists. The phatic function, then, although normally destined to guarantee acoustic reception, reveals through its non-use or misuse the speaker's attitude toward this message as well as toward his listener. Attention to its operation can thus clarify the terms of difference between character and spectator.

The metalinguistic function of language seeks to assure speaker and listener that they share the same linguistic system; its most common use is to ascertain the linguistic competence of an interlocutor for a certain "langue." Yet even where the same code is shared, both speaker and listener often experience the need for clarification. This clarification may be phonetic, morphological, syntactic, or semantic, but it is in no way a *development* of the message in question. The metalinguistic equation is not a commutation among paradigmatic structures, as is the case in the creation of metaphor. Jakobson has emphasized this difference between metalanguage and poetic metaphor, two opposing operations which may often share a similar grammatical form:

> Entre la poésie et le métalangage, toutefois, il y a une opposition diamétrale: *dans le métalangage, la séquence est utilisée pour construire une équation tandis qu'en poésie c'est l'équation qui sert à construire la séquence.*[25]

As was the case with the phatic function, the use or non-use of metalinguistic clarifications implies a certain assessment by the speaker of his listener's relationship to the code they supposedly share. This assessment may or may not be correct in the spectator's judgment; he would find it extremely ridiculous, for example, if an economist interrupted his own speech to a group of his peers in order to define the words "supply" and "demand," however correct the definition. In fact, he would be more inclined to see this superfluousness as a symptom of an exaggerated self-concept. Where repeated explanations of this type were proffered or demanded, any message would lose its efficacity proportionately, since it would be reduced to a series of unnecessary definitions.

Our analysis of the comic violation of this function will center on its designed misuse by a speaker and its unconscious acceptance as deductive interpretation by a listener. Just as the repeated use of phatic expressions could be used to divert a listener's *attention* from the inadequacy of a particular message, the metalinguistic function can often serve to give the impression of regard for listener *comprehension* where no such regard exists. Thus, in *Le Médecin malgré lui*, Sganarelle repeatedly asks Géronte if he is following his absurd medical reasoning, knowing that the latter could not possibly understand. Sganarelle even offers translations, but only for words which have no importance:

---

[25] Jakobson, pp. 220–221.

Sganarelle: Entendez-vous le latin?

Géronte: En aucune façon.

Sganarelle: . . . singulariter, nominativo haec Musa, «la Muse,» . . . Etiam, «oui.» Quare, «pour quoi»? . . . . (II, iv.)

The purpose here is evidently to assure Géronte's *incomprehension*, rather than to define terms in the interest of clarity.

The notion of metalanguage can be extended further to include a certain type of response to reality which seeks, and is satisfied with, only this simplistic definition of terms. *Le Bourgeois Gentilhomme* examines the nature of such a system as well as its evident inadequacies. Moreover, the metalinguistic fallacy may be an important aspect of the classical system of language which sought knowledge in classification and definition. By emphasizing "la forme de l'expression" of any system of meaning, such a system would merely substitute one code for another in a piece-meal fashion, presenting circularity as deduction and denying all but the most superficial types of knowledge.

Whereas the metalinguistic function seeks to ensure the possibility of correct decoding by a listener, the referential, or denotative, function seeks to inform this listener of those particular elements of the situational and/or verbal context a speaker desires to communicate. In the case of abstract discussion, for example, the context to be assured is often solely verbal, as when antecedents must be ordered logically (e.g. celui-ci/celui-là). Where objective reality is directly involved, however, the reference is purely situational, as in "*Voici* l'arbre qui va tomber." In these cases, language serves to verbalize a speaker's perception of external reality in order to communicate it. Benveniste[26] has studied a third type of reference in language found in the use of pronouns: the forms "je" and

---

[26] Emile Benveniste, *Problèmes de linguistique générale* (Paris, 1966), pp. 251–257.

"tu" refer to both the linguistic realities of subject and object and the situational realities of speaker and listener.

In theater, expressions which verbalize the situational context are the spectator's principal source of objective data. These referential data present the particular theatrical reality which each play creates and in reference to which each play develops. Yet apart from certain plays which are preceded by a narration of their actions, or those which use a report to describe actions which occur off-stage, the source of these data is usually first-person monologue or verbal exchanges between characters. Our analysis of comic theater as a text requiring the spectator to decode linguistic signs which have themselves already been encoded and decoded reveals, however, that such data cannot be accepted without suspicion. Such acceptance would place the spectator in the precarious position of being limited to the notion of reality encoded or decoded by one or several characters. This position is potentially destructive of any comic reaction, for it negates the spectator's automatic superior awareness of all theatrical situations. Thus, we often find in comedy efforts to separate character and spectator perception which at times seem unrealistic: one character hiding behind another, for example, or two characters on stage together yet unaware of each other's presence. We will demonstrate, however, that in most instances of such nonperception in Molière, the apparently impossible unconsciousness is actually quite reasonable given the obsessions of the characters involved.

Non-perception of referential reality is perhaps the most obvious source of comic language since the verbal exchanges which result are immediately at variance with the spectator's knowledge of the actual situation. Yet each referential message exchanged on stage codifies at the same time a certain assessment of the referent as well as an *attitude* toward it on the part of a given speaker. In other words, perception in comedy is often a function of desire; certain characters exhibit the tendency to interpret reality as they see fit rather than accept objective data and respond appropriately. The spectator must examine both these aspects, for any difference in perception between him and the character observed can only be formulated in these terms. The "je vois" and the "je veux voir" implicit (at least) in the instances of communication he observes furnish the spectator with his two most important comparative categories.

In the first case, the spectator compares his own perception of a situation with that of the character who verbalizes: Is this really what is happening? On what type of perception is it based (hear-say, direct observance, etc.)? How adequate are these sources? Similar questions are raised in regard to the respondent: Is this really what was referred to? How and why was this particular perception accepted or rejected? If we consider X as the situation topic of discussion, then

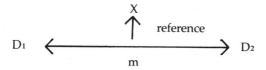

where $D_1(X)$ would be the speaker's perception of the situation and $D_2[D_1(X)]$, the respondent's assessment of this perception revealed by his acceptance or rejection of it. Both of these judgments are directly presented to the spectator, $S[D_1(X)]$ and $S D_2[D_1(X)]$, yielding comparisons between spectator and speaker, as well as between spectator and respondent.

In the case of interference by desire in the perception of referential reality, the instances of communication in any play gradually result in a discrepancy between a character's perception of the action and the spectator's perception. As the latter's broadens, he becomes capable of dissociating himself from a reliance on one character's particular interpretation.

41

The result of this dissociation is a questioning of the latter's judgment, thereby creating the possibility to decide which actions are merely the fantasy of the principal character. More importantly, where both spectator and character would agree on the *fact* of a certain action, the former can decide how this action is wrongly interpreted. In this decision, the spectator becomes aware of a particular character's motivations and the effect of these motivations on the character's perception, or misperception, of reality.

Such comparisons in comedy between character and spectator result in the clarification of the latter's decoding superiority. Not only is his perception of the situation greater than that of the character he observes, but he realizes that the character's deficiency in this area is a direct result of his eccentric desire. In farce, character perception seems almost exclusively derived from such desires: the characters of *Le Cocu imaginaire*, for example, create the entire reality of their play through their desire to prove mutual suspicions. In *L'Ecole des maris*, Sganarelle attempts to present his possessiveness as a logical system conforming to the exigencies of reality; his desire for self-justification, however, belies the theoretical value of his system and reveals that it is merely a rationalized theory in the service of ego-protection. Desire, then, often conflicts with perception and guarantees the spectator's superiority, since only he can understand the interference of one with the other. The spectator's comic reaction, therefore, seems to require an unconsciousness on the part of the character he observes. The non-perception of reality is thus the source of quiproquo's and unconscious self-betrayal which emphasize a particular character's isolation from the theatrical world with which he must deal effectively if he is to avoid manipulation.

Our analysis of language's phatic, metalinguistic, and referential functions has enabled us to examine three important prerequisites for message-reception and correct decoding. Where these requirements are not respected, for whatever reason, the communicative process is aborted. This failure to communicate is not automatically comic, yet each violation contributes to this failure and determines a particular aspect of spectator superiority. A character's awareness of the reception of his message, expressed in his acceptance/violation of the phatic necessity, creates the possibility of comparison between

D_1 : assumed contact vs. S : actual contact/non-contact

His metalinguistic clarifications evoke comparisons between

D_1 : assumed competence of D_2 vs. S : actual competence of D_2

as well as between[27]

competence of D_1 vs. competence of S

Finally, a speaker's denotative ability, as well as his personal assessment of his listener's denotative ability, are revealed in those structures which refer to the factual data to be communicated. Thus his referential expressions evoke comparisons between

D_1 : assumed perception of X by D_2

vs.

S : actual perception of X by D_2

as well as between

perception of X by D_1 vs. perception of X by S

perception of X by D_2 vs. perception of X by S

Our discussion of the referential aspect of language, however, led us to the realization that perception is often

---

[27] By "competence" here we understand the ability to produce and comprehend phonetically, grammatically, and semantically correct statements. For the different types of linguistic competence, see Robin Campbell and Roger Wales, "The Study of Language Acquisition," reprinted in *New Horizons in Linguistics*, ed. John Lyons (Great Britain, 1970), pp. 242–260.

modified by desire. We would distinguish between two different types of such modification where, on one hand, desire results in a total *misrepresentation* of reality, and on the other, desire provokes a *misinterpretation* of reality. In *Le Cocu imaginaire*, Sganarelle's wife finds a portrait of a man, Lélie, which, we are told, she proceeds to smell; Sganarelle, who would love to prove his wife's infidelity, actually *sees* her kiss it, or so he would like to believe. This fundamental interference of desire with objective perception is clearly presented to the spectator who is always aware of the difference between actual and assumed reality. In *Tartuffe*, however, the reality of the hypocrite's actions, going to church, wearing a hairshirt, etc., are perceived in the same way by all; the cause for dispute between Orgon and his family lies in their interpretation.

We must emphasize, in agreeing with Jakobson, that every message implicates in one way or another all three of the functions we have just analyzed, as well as those which refer to speaker sentiment (emotive), to listener effect (conative), and to the message itself (poetic).[28] Yet just as there are types of communication which emphasize one function over another, there would seem to be certain instances of comic language which emphasize the inadequate use of one function over another. We propose to accept this hypothesis as our principle of organization in this study, assuming that a certain type of play will involve one or several of these functions almost to the exclusion of others. We have already indicated the apparent connection between farce and the phatic, metalinguistic, and referential functions of communication. Before we can examine more extensive plays such as *Tartuffe, George Dandin,* and *Le Misanthrope*, we must investigate the role of speaker, listener, and message in the creation of the comic.

---

[28] v. p. 214:
   "La diversité de messages réside non dans le monopole de l'une ou l'autre fonction, mais dans les différences de hiérarchie entre celles-ci. La structure verbale d'un message dépend avant tout de la fonction prédominante."

IV. Persuasion and the Comic

Let us return, then, to an instance of communication, assuming the presence of two interlocutors who are in aural/oral contact, who are equally competent linguistically, and who respectively encode and decode adequately the denotative information transmitted. Let us assume further that the first speaker (D₁) attempts to convince his listener (D₂) of a particular interpretation of this objective information in order to evoke a response appreciative of his desires. This act of persuasion involves both a method and a motive, a type of discursive logic and a purpose which this logic must serve, either explicitly or implicitly. From the spectator's point of view, however, and at times from the listener's as well if he is aware that he is being persuaded, any discourse used by the speaker is simultaneously *action* and *symptom*: action in the sense that it seeks to effect a particular response, yet symptom in that it remains in at least implicit relation to the desire it would satisfy.

Where a speaker expects or encounters no disagreement, he is likely to express his desires explicitly and consequently, his discourse-as-action is presented to the spectator for objective evaluation. Thus its efficacity is determinable by comparing the response it should logically evoke according to the spectator with that which it actually evokes from the listener. Where the spectator's hypothetical response is logically compatible with the listener's actual one, the spectator may conclude that the message *as formulated* was effective; what was explicitly asked for was produced. In comedy, however, explicit statements are the exception rather than the rule. Their use implies a certain attitude on the part of their speaker toward his desire—that it is obviously justifiable—and toward his listener—that the latter will accept it as such and respond accordingly. The situation becomes much more complex, however, in the case of disagreement.

Where disagreement is either expected from the outset or indicated by the first responses obtained, the speaker finds himself obliged to demonstrate the correctness of his particular interpretation. Conversely, where such logical demonstration is impossible, he must dissimulate in such a way that the illogicalness of his interpretation is indiscernible. In either case, however, such demonstration or dissimulation can only be accomplished by formulations which would be comprehensible to, and interpreted in a certain way by, the given listener. Yet since the spectator is involved here as well, this "rhetoric" is judged according to its use or misuse of logical principles, as well as according to the effectiveness of its dissimulation. Thus, although a certain discursive logic may be quite acceptable to a given listener, therefore evoking a response satisfactory to the speaker, this same logic may be completely inadequate from the spectator's point of view. Any instance of discursive persuasion, then, enables the spectator to formulate judgments about the cognitive capabilities of both speaker and listener. Leaving aside for the moment the complex question of how much a given speaker is himself convinced by his own logic, the following combinations seem possible:

(i)	Spectator and listener convinced
(ii)	Listener convinced/spectator unconvinced
(iii)	Spectator convinced/listener unconvinced
(iv)	Spectator and listener unconvinced

Each of these possibilities defines a certain type of relationship between "fourbe," "fou," and spectator which must be examined in order to determine how language's potentially persuasive power may become comic. Let us investigate each by referring to a specific example from Molière.

One of the central issues of the debate over *Tartuffe* involved the criticism leveled by certain "dévots" against the play. The nature of this criticism was perfectly clear to Molière:

> On me reproche d'avoir mis des termes de piété dans la bouche de mon imposteur. Eh! pouvais-je m'en empêcher, pour bien représenter le caractère d'un hypocrite? Il suffit, ce me semble, que je fasse connaître les motifs criminels qui lui font dire les choses . . . .[29]

The problem with Tartuffe, then, was that for some, he was too convincing; his words, which he shared with "vrais" and "faux dévots" alike, made it appear that he was actually "vrai." Such a judgment based solely on Tartuffe's *explicit* formulations indicates a total insensibility to his *implied* motives. This is ironically exactly Orgon's problem as well, who at least has the excuse that he does not observe *all* of Tartuffe's theatrical activity. It is evident that for any spectator who believes in Tartuffe as Orgon does, this play could not possibly evoke a comic reaction. Despite all Molière's attention to Tartuffe's self-betrayal, despite all his insistence on the clear vision of all characters except Orgon and Madame Pernelle, wherever identification exists between dupe and spectator, the comic evaporates as the latter's decoding superiority is rendered inoperable.

---

[29] Molière, "Préface," in *Oeuvres complètes*, ed. Robert Jouanny (Paris, 1962), p. 630. All future page references are to this edition.

An even more problematic case arises where all listeners are unconvinced yet the spectator himself *is* convinced. This difference between listener and spectator, and the consequent identification of speaker and spectator, may be the key to our difficulty in judging *Le Misanthrope* comic. With the possible exception of Eliante, the society against which Alceste revolts is supremely worthy of the exposure he continually forces upon it. This may also be the case with *George Dandin,* although cetainly on a lower moral level. Neither Alceste nor Dandin inhabit a problematic world; the insincerity of society and the unfaithfulness of Angélique are incontrovertible facts as clear to the characters involved as they are to the spectator. The principal benefit of our attention to the implicit, however, is that it affords us the means to judge both Alceste and Dandin with respect to the inconsistencies their own use of language betrays. We will indicate the process by which such judgments can be made when we examine the question of a speaker's consciousness of the connotative implications inherent to his formulations. Such an examination will emphasize the distinction between the actual situation described by the entire play, insincerity or infidelity, and the particular interpretation of and reaction to this situation on the part of the principal character. This distinction seems crucial for any comic reaction, for if spectator and character interpretations do not differ significantly, if the former is not more aware of the actual situation than the latter, the comic again becomes impossible.

In the situation where the listener is convinced while the spectator is not, the speaker involved has evidently succeeded in exploiting a particular susceptibility in his listener which the spectator does not share. Such a situation seems to be the purest comic presentation, for it allows the spectator to separate himself by his superior decoding ability from the character deceived. An obvious example would be *Le Médecin volant,* where Sganarelle convinces Gorgibus that he is a renowned doctor with the following "logical" discourse:

Sganarelle:	. . . car, par exemple, comme la mélancholie est ennemie de la joie, et que la bile qui se répand par le corps nous fait devenir jaunes, et qu'il n'est rien plus contraire à la santé que la maladie, nous pouvons dire . . . que votre fille est fort malade. Il faut que je vous fasse une ordonnance.
Gorgibus:	Vite, une table, du papier, de l'encre! (p. 27)

Such credulousness on the part of characters like Gorgibus is often simply arbitrarily given as part of their nature, yet it may just as often appear as the direct result of demonstrated linguistic inadequacies within this character's speech-system. Where such demonstration occurs, as in *Le Bourgeois Gentilhomme*, the impression of rigorous psycholinguistic presentation on Molière's part is created, and the notion of comic justice is joined to the play's particular moral of language.

Our final possibility involves cases where both listener and spectator are unconvinced. The clearest example of this situation would be *L'Ecole des maris*, where Sganarelle's precepts on child education are effectively debated by Ariste and cleverely circumvented by Valère and Isabelle. The spectator is invited to conclude that Sganarelle operates within a self-imposed system of isolation totally at variance with the reality that surrounds him. His power over Isabelle is so obviously arbitrary and so clearly presented as self-indulgence that it becomes supremely appropriate that he should be overcome by feigned submission to it. Molière seems to reach technical perfection in this play by deftly interweaving Sganarelle's self-complacency and self-betrayal in making of him both the agent and the object of his defeat.

Let us formalize the nature of the discursive logic we have been considering as method of persuasion and symptom of desire. Disagreement is evident whenever the spectator observes a situation where a certain expression (E), which explicitly encodes a certain desire (D_S), evokes instead a response other than the satisfaction of this desire. In order to remedy this situation, the speaker is obliged to formulate a modified desire (D'_S) in such a way that its correspondingly modified expression (E') might evoke a satisfactory response (D'_R). Yet at the same time, this modified expression (E') must serve the same purpose as the original (E) while not appearing to. This implies as well, however, that D_S and D'_S are related in a way similar to E and E'. Where such a process succeeds, we would observe

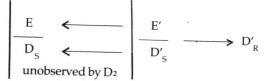

The union of E' and D'_S represents a compromise, then, between the explicit statement (E) of desire (D_S) and the type of satisfactory response (D'_R) possible to obtain from the listener in question. Let us examine how such dissimulation operates in Molière, insisting specifically on examples of its justifiable and unjustifiable use.

Cléonte's difficulty with Monsieur Jourdain in *Le Bourgeois Gentilhomme* furnishes an excellent example of our theory. Seeking to gain Jourdain's compliance for marrying his daughter, Cléonte first apologizes for the fact that he is not a "gentilhomme." The response he obtains reveals how explicit desire, even when acceptable, can meet with failure when it confronts the arbitrary whims of its desired respondent:

> Cléonte: . . . je trouve que toute imposture est indigne d'un honnête homme, et qu'il y a de la lâcheté à déguiser ce que le Ciel nous a fait naître . . . à se vouloir donner pour ce qu'on n'est pas . . . et je vous dirai franchement que je ne suis point gentilhomme.
>
> Jourdain: Touchez là, Monsieur, ma fille n'est pas pour vous. (p. 484)

It is evident that Cléonte speaks from the heart here and that he believes his honesty will impress Jourdain enough to overcome his lack of nobility. This is clearly not the case, for Cléonte's explicit expression of honesty (E), which formulates univocally his desire (D_s), is met instead by a negative response. Cléonte can succeed only by hiding his true nature and masquerading as someone who would *honor* Jourdain by accepting his daughter. We can outline this as follows:

$$\left|\begin{array}{c} E \;:\; \text{honesty} \\ \hline D_S \quad \text{acceptance} \end{array}\right. \xleftarrow{} \left|\begin{array}{c} E' \;:\; \text{"Turkish" dishonesty} \xrightarrow{} \text{acceptance} : D'_R \\ \hline D'_S \qquad \text{magnanimity} \end{array}\right.$$

As will be the case with Tartuffe, Cléonte depends on hypocrisy to effect the desired response. While it is clear that he is therefore no longer qualified to speak of his honesty, this loss is attributed specifically to Jourdain's obsessions, which dictate the behavior of all who would circumvent them. Cléonte's honesty, then, would actually be comic if he persisted in light of evidence that Jourdain cannot be dealt with in this way. By expressing himself honestly first, however, Cléonte enlists the sympathy of the spectator, who therefore finds any subsequent dishonesty more a judgment of Jourdain than of its perpetrator.

Masquerade is perhaps the most obvious persuasive technique and as such the easiest for the spectator to uncover. Depending on the credulousness of one's listener, anyone can assume a more powerful identity. Yet manipulating reality in this way is dangerous, since appearances are less controllable to the degree that they depend on tangible modifications of physical reality. This is the key to Sganarelle's unmasking in *Le Médecin volant*, where manipulation by objects is ultimately confronted by the objects themselves. Most of Molière's "fourbes" play this game in a more subtle way, depending on words alone to create the desired effect. Scapin is excellent at this technique, but Tartuffe is clearly the master of it, at least as far as Orgon is concerned. Accused by Damis, Tartuffe replies to Orgon:

Croyez ce qu'on vous *dit*, armez votre courroux,
Et comme un criminel *chassez*-moi de chez vous. (p. 676)

51

The procedure is clear to the spectator:

$$
\begin{array}{|l|l|}
\hline
\text{E} \ : \ \text{Ne croyez pas. . .} \quad \longleftarrow \ \text{E}' \ : & \text{croyez. . .} \qquad \text{Orgon le} \ : \ \text{D}_\text{R} \\
\hline
\text{D}_\text{S} \quad \text{gardez-moi} \quad \longleftarrow \ \text{D}'_\text{S} & \text{Chassez-moi} \qquad \overset{\longrightarrow}{\text{garde}} \\
\hline
\end{array}
$$

Tartuffe's control of Orgon is so complete that he can even modify his real desire (D_S) to the point of saying its opposite, D'_S. This is accomplished by creating an identification between banishment and belief in the words of another. Realizing that Orgon depends on no one but himself for the "truth," Tartuffe thus succeeds in assuring his continued acceptance. Unfortunately for Tartuffe, any intelligent spectator can see the implications of such logic. If the modified desire (D'_S) is the negative of the real desire (D_S), then the modified expression (E') must also be the negative of an implied original expression (E). The latter, then, would be "Ne croyez pas ce qu'on vous dit," yet what Damis tells Orgon is a *fact* observed by Damis and the spectator alike. It is clear, therefore, that in believing Tartuffe, Orgon demonstrates his disbelief in factual reality when the expression of this reality conflicts with what he wants to believe. Where the character deceived remains in control of others, however, the play must be resolved from without. In this case, Tartuffe's game will be ended by the King who *will* believe in what others tell him:

> Et par un juste trait de l'équité suprême,
> S'est découvert au Prince un fourbe renommé,
> Dont sous un autre nom il était informé . . . (p. 705)

Persuasive speech, then, relies on the use of implication in order to evoke indirectly the satisfaction of a particular desire. For our purposes, the most important item in this process is *what is not said* (E). What is the reason for such dissimulation and how does it affect the communicative process? Ducrot has indicated several possible motives, of which we find one particularly relevant to our discussion:

Une seconde origine possible au besoin d'implicite tient au fait que toute affirmation explicitée devient, par cela même, un thème de discussion. *Tout ce qui est dit peut être contredit.* De sorte qu'on ne saurait annoncer une opinion ou un désir, sans les désigner du même coup aux objections éventuelles des interlocuteurs.[30]

The implicit in Ducrot's analysis, then, appears as a deviation from the normal transference of information; it seeks to continue the effectiveness of the desires it hides without explicitly presenting these desires for discussion, and therefore possible rejection. The choice to speak implicitly, therefore, is actually an implied judgment of the acceptability of these desires. This judgment may be generated by the realization that such desires are in themselves unjustifiable, or by the knowledge that their listener would certainly consider them as such.

The spectator of comedy often finds himself confronted by this implicit language, for the characters he observes seem forever involved in dissimulating arbitrary patterns of encoding or circumventing arbitrary patterns of decoding. His role in such a system must be to uncover what is not said and determine if the reason for such dissimulation lies in the unacceptability of the desire dissimulated or in the arbitrary refusal of this desire on the part of the respondent. At times, this task is relatively simple: the speaker himself often betrays unwittingly the arbitrariness of his desires or is adroitly manipulated into so doing by a skillful "fourbe." In certain cases, however, uncovering the implicit is a much more difficult task, since it is often necessary to contrast the desire expressed with the form of its expression. In the case of *George Dandin*, for example, the principal character reveals a fundamental inconsistency in his language: while reproaching his wife for appreciating him not as a person but rather as a certain sum of money, Dandin betrays the fact that he considers *himself* as this certain sum. Thus, he is placed in the ridiculous position of condemning others for accepting him *as he unwittingly presents himself.* This

---

[30] Oswald Ducrot, *Dire et ne pas dire* (Paris, 1972), p. 6.

factor brings us to our final methodological consideration: the relationship which a particular character perceives (or does not perceive) between what he believes he is saying and the implicit connotative consequences of this speech.

It appears extremely difficult to determine exactly a given speaker's consciousness of what his speech actually expresses, since this speech is normally reactive and may depend more on the communicative context than on any particular obsession. Yet theater in general, and comedy in particular, differ from this everyday reality in that these contexts are specifically chosen in order to facilitate the revelation of eccentric obsessions. The comic fool, moreover, reveals a certain similarity of responses to varying stimuli and thus often exposes a consistent structure of perception. Wherever such structures are revealed, the spectator is confronted by a choice: either they are consciously chosen by the character observed, in which case their motivation must be determined, or they represent an unconsciousness on the part of their speaker, in which case they indicate a certain loss of control over his speech. How this loss of control becomes comic will be our present concern.

Consider Dandin's opening monologue, wherein he expresses his resentment of those nobles who would accept him only for his money:

> L'alliance qu'ils font est petite avec nos personnes:
> c'est notre bien seul qu'ils épousent . . . . (p. 189)

An unjust situation, it appears, and one that Dandin is quite justified in resenting, for he is reduced therein to a certain amount of money. Yet in pleading his case before the spectator, Dandin causes the latter's sympathy to evaporate:

> A: . . . et j'aurais bien mieux fait, tout riche que je suis, de m'allier en bonne et franche paysannerie que de prendre une femme qui . . . pense qu'avec tout mon bien je n'ai pas assez acheté la qualité de son mari . . . . (p. 189)

Implicit in this expression is the following assumption:

A':   *Si* je m'étais allié avec une paysanne, j'aurais eu une femme
        qui . . . *ne* pense *pas* que je n'ai pas assez achetè la qualité
        de son mari.

                                or

A":   J'aurais dû m'allier avec une femme qui penserait que
        j'avais assez acheté la qualité de son mari.

Notice that the existence of such a woman is never questioned
nor does Dandin ever consider the possibility that money
might not evoke acceptance. The reason for this is clear:
Dandin believes that his "personne" *should be* appreciated for
his money. These implications contrast strongly with
Dandin's apparent assessment of his situation, and invite the
spectator to doubt its veracity. Since Dandin's purpose here is
evidently self-justification, we would imagine that such implications should never be allowed to present themselves for they
destroy his case. The spectator can only conclude, then, that
Dandin's speech betrays him and that consequently, he is
unaware of what he is actually saying.

    Let us insist on this: implication is a function of logic. Just
as the combining of premises limits the extent of any deductive
sequence, so also the combining of statements specifies the
intention which motivates them. The simple expression:

    A: All my friends came.

when spoken without any additions, automatically implies

        A':   I have friends.
        A":   None of my friends stayed home.
        A"':   Since you did not come, you are not one of my
                friends.

Each of these implications corresponds to a different emphasis, and consequently to a different desire, which may or
may not have been intended. Unless further explicit information is offered, a listener may assume any of them to be operative. By limiting himself to the original expression, any

speaker allows the processes of the implicit to undermine what he actually intends. This process need not be limited to comparing the implications of one expression with the explicit formulation of another, as was the case with Dandin. As we will subsequently show, explicit and implicit may clash in logical absurdity even within a single statement.

In all of Molière's plays, language's implicit potential, even when purposefully exploited, forces its exploiter to live with the logical or illogical structure and content of his dissimulation. He is thus clearly exposed to the spectator who may judge this personal version of logic as well as the perception of reality this logic exposes. To the degree that a given character does not, or refuses to, confront the consequences of his logic and continues in the self-delusion that an intrinsic identity exists between what he says and what he believes he is saying, he exposes himself unwittingly to the arbitrariness of his own desires and reveals his inadequate control over their expression in speech.

What, then, are the requirements for language to become comic, and in what way is our analysis of this comic language important for understanding the moral of language in Molière?

As we demonstrated in our first section, a given character's language is potentially comic only where it is unconsciously or designedly misused. It would be difficult to imagine a comic of correct language; although we may laugh at someone who uses language correctly yet is continually thwarted in the expression of his desires, our laughter in this case is unrelated to the comic per se. Where language is unconsciously misused, we must decide: first, to what degree this misuse is caused by the nature of language itself to escape the control of its speaker; secondly, to what degree this escape is caused by the interference of arbitrary desire in the normal processes of encoding and decoding. Where language is designedly misused, we must examine the effectiveness of this misuse by evaluating the response it evokes.

In our section on the communicative act, we indicated how language can become automatically ineffective where it violates certain prerequisites. Speaking with the belief that one's listener is attentive while he is actually not, speaking with nothing to say yet giving the impression of meaning, speaking incorrectly phonetically, syntactically or semantically, speaking at the same time as someone else—all such situations serve to present a speaker whose linguistic competence is inferior to our own.

In our specific analysis of persuasion, we demonstrated how the necessity to imply rather than express desire indicated a judgment of the speaker's assessment of this desire and/or a judgment of his listener's decoding priorities. Successful persuasion of a listener did not automatically imply that the spectator was also convinced, since the latter was in the position to judge the process of such persuasion and determine the acceptability of the desires it logically implied.

Having considered these aspects of language's use, we can now offer a tentative definition of the comic we will seek to examine in this study.

> The comic of language involves the presentation of significant behaviors
>
> (a) which are determinable by the repetition of similar stimulus-response patterns in the act of communication
>
> (b) through which desires are formulated with the purpose of effecting their satisfaction
>
> (c) and through which characters may unwittingly reveal their motivations
>
> (d) and may betray their individual eccentric preoccupations
>
> (e) to a listener who manipulates or is manipulated by such formulations
>
> (f) and to a spectator who judges himself in some way superior to both speaker and listener

(g) basing his judgment on the comparison of assumed normal competence vs. exhibited performance on the linguistic and discursive levels.

The importance of language in this definition should be evident, for to the degree that speech implicates codal competence, it can be judged by invoking the normative systematicity of language ("langue"). Moreover, the ineffectiveness of any *activity* can be more easily understood by referring to the verbalizations which would seek to communicate the motives of such action and evoke their satisfaction. Finally, the preeminence of language among semiological systems would seem to imply the potential fruitfulness of a linguistic/discursive analysis applied to comedy as a system of meaningful and meaning-seeking behaviors.

Every instance of language's use evidences a re-definition of what it means to speak; every verbal exchange implicates speaker, message, and listener at the same time as it questions the nature of the entire communicative process. To speak, then, is to define oneself with regard to the act of speaking. Wherever speech is observed, therefore, the limits of speaking itself can be discovered. We will attempt to demonstrate that comedy in general, and Molière in particular, seek to examine these limits in a way which would affirm certain implicit theories of communication by ridiculing the inadequacies of others, thus revealing the moral of language use implied by its comic transformation.

Part Two

THE LANGUAGE
OF FARCE

V.   Importance of Farce in Molière

All Molière critics agree that no serious study of Molière's comic theater would be complete without an examination of its farces. Few, however, are prepared to give such a study the primacy we believe it deserves. For the most part, Molière criticism has seemed content to consider this maligned genre as a poor reflection of the later, more "serious," comedies, explaining away its existence by Molière's financial need to create plays rapidly that would appeal to the "parterre."[1] This type of apology misses the point entirely, we believe. Historical consideration of Molière's early exposure to "theater," his early successes, and the triumphs of his later career all indicate the fundamental importance of farce as technique and as aesthetic principle for his evolution as a comic dramatist. This genre and its techniques, presented on the Pont-Neuf or at the Fair of St. Germain under Louis XIII,

---

[1] A notable exception would be Bowen's treatment of farce as a distinctive literary genre. Cf. Barbara Bowen, *Les Caractéristiques essentielles de la farce* (Urbana, 1964).

were the young Molière's first encounter with non-serious theater. There he observed for the first time two traditions which cast their influence over his later work: the French farcic tradition of the Middle Ages with its violence, and the new Italian "commedia dell'arte" with its intricate plots and "recognition" denouements. This early exposure was later complemented during Molière's fourteen-year sojourn in the provinces, a sojourn dedicated to the creation and adaptation of innumerable farces of which, unfortunately, few remain. Moreover, it was the presentation of a farce, *Les Précieuses ridicules*, which marked his first Parisian theatrical success upon his return in 1659. However unreliable the documentation of his life, it is historically undeniable that farce was one of Molière's first interests.

Farce lies not merely chronologically at the origins of Molière's theater, however. The choice of this genre for his earliest dramatic attempts would indicate that Molière felt an affinity for its techniques and perceived therein a certain compatability with his own comic vision. This vision would be later extended far beyond the limitations which farce presented in character portrayal and subject matter, yet it was to remain hidden behind many of the situations of the more serious plays only to burst forth where least expected. We need only think of Alain and Georgette with their "potage," Orgon under a table, Dandin stumbling around in the darkness, or Sganarelle bemoaning the loss of his salary to verify this. Lanson has demonstrated the continuity of this farcic vision throughout the later comedies as an aesthetic principle which was ceaselessly evolving by its contact with varied dramatic situations while remaining true to its basic principles:

> Farce is at the root of all Molière's comedy, even in its highest forms, the comedy of manners and the comedy of character . . . upon the trunk of farce was grafted everything his superior genius invented through an original vision of life, every seriousness and profundity his robust and free mind introduced into these hilarious images of the ridiculous. And it is by the *cultiva-*

tion, by the *transformation* of farce that Molière came to those masterpieces that seem furthest from farce.[2] (Italics ours)

One of our major tasks will be to demonstrate the pertinence of this remark and the vast consequences of this union of farce and comedy for any understanding of Molière's more difficult plays.

We find ourselves on solid ground, then, historically and aesthetically, when we choose farce as our departure point. This choice appears even more sound from a methodological point of view. Farce has often been considered a rudimentary form of comedy and, while we believe that as a genre it evidences distinctive aesthetic principles, we nevertheless might expect to find the problems posed by comedy to be presented in farce in an elementary way. We find in several cases, for example, a farce coupled with a three-act comedy wherein the elementary farcic situations are developed into a more profound social and psychological context, as in the case of *La Jalousie du Barbouillé—George Dandin* and *Le Médecin volant—Le Médecin malgré lui*. Thematic echoes of this type enable the critic to trace more adequately the frontier between farce and comedy.

More important for our particular method of linguistic/ psychological analysis, however, is the possibility to observe the comic use of language at its origins and to indicate its evolution through the more sophisticated comedies. We might expect to find the elementary nature of farcic action and character portrayal reflected in, and in a certain sense, created by, the confrontation between speech-systems which are just as elementary. The inadequacies these confrontations demonstrate should indicate violations of the fundamental prerequisites of message-communicability which we outlined in our methodological section. Just as the psychologist of language

---

[2] Gustave Lanson, "Molière and Farce," in *Comedy: Meaning and Form*, ed. Robert Corrigan (Scranton, 1965), p. 380.

begins with the language of the child then, the psychologist of comic language would do well to begin with the language of farce; if the child's first use of language is purely accessory, as Piaget has demonstrated,[3] it seems quite possible that farcic language may also be defined by virtue of its total disregard for communicability. There seems no better place to begin an analysis of the misuses of language, then, than where these misuses are most fundamental.

---

[3] Jean Piaget, *The Language and Thought of the Child*, trans. Marjorie Gabain (New York, 1971), pp. 25–30.

VI.   Le Mariage forcé

> La parole a été donnée à l'homme pour
> expliquer sa pensée; et tout ainsi que
> les pensées sont les portraits des
> choses, de même nos paroles sont-elles
> les portraits de nos pensées; mais ces
> portraits diffèrent des autres portraits
> en ce que les autres portraits sont
> distingués partout de leurs originaux,
> et que la parole enferme en soi son
> original, puisqu'elle n'est autre chose
> que la pensée expliquée par un signe
> extérieur: d'où vient que ceux qui
> pensent bien sont aussi ceux qui
> parlent le mieux. Expliquez-moi donc
> votre pensée par la parole, qui est le
> plus intelligible de tous les signes.[4]

This passage from one of Molière's less familiar farces contains as much overt linguistic theory as will be found in his

---

[4] Pancrace, in *Le Mariage forcé*, sc. iv, in *Molière: Oeuvres complètes*, ed. Robert Jouanny (Paris, 1962), pp. 560–561. All future page references are to this edition unless otherwise indicated.

theater. As an orderly, logical presentation of the relationships between thought, speech, and object, it can be criticized for little more than its oversimplification and pedantry. While masking certain problematic areas with vague terms, "portraits," "originaux," "signe extérieur," it nevertheless succeeds in impressing the reader with its apparent lucidity. Moreover, as numerous annotators of this play have remarked, its speaker's philosophical contentions are elsewhere correctly formulated, leading us to believe that there is some truth to this particular explanation.[5] We will demonstrate in a later section how Molière's use of comic language destroys the simplicity of this view, but as a text, apart from its pedantic form, there seems to be little reason to consider it ridiculous. Yet this particular scene is a masterpiece of farcic technique. A different type of operation must be at work here, one which we believe is profoundly farcic, as opposed to comic, an operation which will enable us to effect a preliminary separation between the comic and farcic misuses of language.

The key to the farcic effect of Pancrace's words on the importance of speech for the communication of thought lies in the timing of their delivery: Pancrace speaks "en même temps que Sganarelle." Thus, his words never even reach his supposed listener; he condemns them to incommunicability from the outset. This violation of what Jakobson[6] and others have called the phatic function of speech, that function which serves to guarantee the contact between speaker and listener which is a prerequisite for any communication, is perhaps the most obvious of farcic techniques.[7] In this particular case, it indicates Pancrace's belief in the self-sufficiency of his lan-

---

[5] v Jouanny's notes on the play, nos. 679, 682, p. 917.

[6] Roman Jakobson, "Linguistique et poétique," reprinted in *Essais de linguistique générale* (Paris, 1963), p. 217.

[7] We would also note that any reference to this function is significantly absent from Pancrace's theory of communication.

guage, a language for which a listener is considered superfluous. This violation of an elementary rule of communication
is repeatedly exploited under various forms throughout the
play—gratuitous interruption, non-sequitur—in order to
formulate and satirize the abnormal use of language as a type
of self-administered acoustic stimulus. That language for
Pancrace is just such an auto-stimulus is clear from the sequence of rejoinders immediately preceding our original
quote:

Pancrace:	*Expliquez* donc *votre pensée*, car je ne puis pas la deviner.
Sganarelle:	Je vous la veux expliquer aussi, mais il faut m'écouter.
Sganarelle:	(en même temps que le Docteur) L'affaire que j'ai à vous dire . . .
Pancrace:	(en même temps que Sganarelle) La parole a été donnée à l'homme pour *expliquer sa pensée* . . . (p. 560).

Thus instead of cuing himself from Sganarelle's expression of
his desire to communicate a problem, Pancrace responds to his
own problem, the explanation of communication in general.
The simultaneity of this explanation with Sganarelle's question destroys the process of communication at its most fundamental step, namely the *linear* transmission and exchange of
utterances. As Saussure has demonstrated in his concept of
"le circuit de la parole," in normal conversation, speakers
exchange statements in a series wherein each is alternately
speaker and listener.[8] The communication of meaning is possible only where these *successive* statements do not interfere
with each other. For Pancrace, however, this successivity is

---

[8] Ferdinand de Saussure, *Cours de linguistique générale*, édition critique,
ed. Tulio de Mauro (Paris, 1972), p. 28. We will subsequently explain how this
explanation is inadequate wherever factors are introduced which impede the
process by which a given concept evokes a corresponding acoustic image,
factors such as dissimulation and loss of control.

merely between statements of his own articulation and could, at the limit, guarantee only self-communication. There is even further irony here, however: by declaring that speech is essential for communication *at the same time as* he denies Sganarelle the very possibility of speech, Pancrace betrays a disregard for the meaning of his own words. Thus his discourse loses all meaning, affecting neither listener nor speaker except insofar as it stimulates more self-directed discourse from the same source. It becomes a rather curious speech, stripped of all communicability and divested of all but the quality of perpetuating itself ineffectively.

Our analysis of the preceding passages has demonstrated the importance of context for the determination of the comic effect. Pancrace's speech, though it manifested no incongruity either in meaning or expression, became comic by virtue of its inadequacy for the situational context in which it was presented. We will attempt to expand gradually this notion of context, first to the entire scene in question, and then to the total play. In the first case, we will be able to understand more clearly the abnormal nature of Pancrace's linguistic system; in the second, Sganarelle's system and the reasons for its failure.

Pancrace's misuse of language surprises Sganarelle, who has failed to comprehend the first part of this scene, yet it does not escape the spectator. The latter has earlier observed Pancrace concluding (or so it seemed) a philosophical argument with an adversary over whether one must say "la figure" or "la forme d'un chapeau." The argument was apparently finished as far as this adversary was concerned, but Pancrace had not yet finished with him, choosing rather to continue the dispute after his listener had departed. The lack of effect on Pancrace of this absence of his interlocutor emphasizes his ability to proceed without one, and supports our judgment of his "conversation" with Sganarelle.

The inadequacy of Pancrace's use of language can be seen primarily in his choice of abnormal paradigmatic modifications in several syntagmatic constructions. The first of these, ". . . vous êtes . . . un homme bannissable de la république des lettres" (p. 554), when taken alone, indicates no aberration. "La république des lettres," though pedantic, is an acceptable substitution for "l'ensemble des gens de lettres." In Dubois'[9] terminology, this metaphor requires disregarding the seme "geographical extension" in order to emphasize the mutual semes of "order" and "governance" on the basis of which the comparison is founded. Even the word "bannissable" is allowable here, for it admits of the same possible disregard.[10] The comparison becomes ridiculous, however, when Pancrace adds: "une proposition condamnable dans toutes les terres de la philosophie" (p. 555). The word "terres" does not admit *as readily* of disregard for geographical extension and as such, re-introduces in this case the seme disallowed in the creation of the first comparison. Le Guern has established the comic nature of such extended metaphors:

> Tout le comique de la phrase vient de ce
> que l'enchaînement apparemment logique des
> deux métaphores est inconciliable avec la
> logique du processus métaphorique. Il est
> produit par le fonctionnement du langage
> lui-même puisque la nature des réalités
> désignées n'a rien qui puisse susciter le
> rire ou le sourire.[11]

While comic in their semantic incongruity, these metaphors nevertheless have a further effect. By associating the metaphoric process with the more fundamental process of the

---

[9] Jacques Dubois, *Rhétorique générale* (Paris, 1970), pp. 106ff.

[10] e.g. "banni de mon coeur."

[11] Michel LeGuern, *Sémantique de la métaphore et de la métonymie* (Paris, 1973), p. 16.

discernment of similarity, Jakobson[12] has prepared the way for an analysis of the structures of personal perception through an investigation of their metaphoric expression in speech. Through his use and misuse of metaphor, then, Pancrace betrays a perception of reality which is patently abnormal. Erudition is the common denominator of his imagined society which, in Pancrace's mind, has become a physical reality. The behavior of its primary inhabitant is indeed singular:

> P: Je crèverois plutôt que d'avouer ce que
> tu dis . . . . (p. 555)

That is, that violent death is preferable to accepting an erroneous proposition. Even the physical constitution of its inhabitants is curious:

> P: . . . je soutiendrai mon opinion jusqu'à
> la dernière goutte de mon *encre*. (p. 555)

The last substitution of "encre" for "sang" in the expression "la dernière goutte de mon sang" seems to indicate that for Pancrace, ink has replaced blood as the life-force of his being.

Pancrace's inability to control his language reveals itself more clearly in his tendency to create and extend syntagms by the insertion of curious paradigmatic series. The first of these constructions involves the use of a grammatical paradigm to insult an adversary:

> P: . . . tu es un ignorant, ignorantissime,
> ignorantifiant et ignorantifié par
> tous les cas et modes imaginables. (p. 555)

whereas the second is based on phonic similarity:

> P: . . . un ignorant m'a voulu soutenir
> une proposition *erronée*, une propo-
> sition *épouvantable, effroyable,
> exécrable*. (p. 556)

---

[12] Roman Jakobson, "Deux aspects de langage et deux types d'aphasie," in *Essais*, pp. 43–67.

These formulations support our first conclusion that Pancrace's speech is self-propagating. When he is angered, one of his words can generate a series of similar forms, grammatical and/or phonic, which extend the syntagm in question while adding nothing to its meaning. Each series, however, indicates a particular inadequate understanding of the relationship between linguistic structures and the concepts they would explain. In the first series, "ignorant, etc.," Pancrace reveals his belief that an adversary's ignorance can be more forcefully proven to the degree that it admits of extension to further grammatical cases and modes. It is evident to any spectator, however, that ignorance in the nominative is the same as ignorance in the accusative, for example, and therefore that grammatical extension does not imply semantic or emphatic extension. The second series, "erronée, épouvant*able*, *ef*froy*able*, *ex*éc*rable*," motivated by phonetic similarity, would imply that a mistaken proposition can evoke a feeling of physical disgust and terror. It seems, however, that given the original topic of debate, "la forme ou la figure d'un chapeau," this series of affective responses is at total variance with the normal reaction to an erroneous proposition. The spectator is invited to conclude, then, that Pancrace is merely stringing out synonyms with no regard for the concept they would clarify. In short, that Pancrace's linguistic system develops content according to similarity of form.

Our analysis of Pancrace's linguistic habits has demonstrated how a method of psychological deduction from observed speech facilitates the study of cognitive structures. To this point, however, we have been examining Pancrace's aberrations solely from the perspective of the spectator. In order to understand the position of such a speech-system in the play, we must now examine how Sganarelle reacts to it.

Although Pancrace betrays a thoroughly incompetent use of language in the presence of Sganarelle, the latter is unable to exploit these inadequacies in any way. Despite his success, albeit limited, in gaining the Doctor's attention with such words as "Monsieur le Docteur," "Seigneur Aristote," and "Vous avez raison," expressions which penetrate Pancrace's self-stimulating language, Sganarelle is unable to effectively adapt his language to that of his desired listener. The result of this confrontation between two unmodified "discours" is a return to the original situation with no gain on the part of either speaker. Yet it is certainly Sganarelle who is manipulated here, for although it is clear to the spectator that no communication is possible with Pancrace except on his own terms, Sganarelle nevertheless persists. He is forced to submit to numerous "cérémonies" wherein Pancrace offers him the choice of ten languages, all of which are unknown to Sganarelle. This manipulation of the *form* of his conversation is extended further to a control of its *content*: Pancrace follows his enumeration of acceptable languages with the choice of eight philosophical topics on which he will allow discussion. Sganarelle's final attempt falls victim to Pancrace's unawareness of his own words, expressed this time by a classic farcic technique:

P: Je vous écoute, parlez.
S: Je dis donc, Monsieur le Docteur, que . . .
P: Mais soyez surtout bref.
S: Je le serai.
P: Evitez la prolixité.
S: Hé! Monsi . . .
P: Tranchez-moi votre discours d'un apophtegme
   à la laconienne.
S: Je vous . . .
P: Point d'ombrages, de circonlocution.

(Sganarelle, de dépit de ne pouvoir parler,
ramasse des pierres pour en casser la tête
du Docteur). (pp. 561–562)

The comic here again lies in the incongruity between the expression and the content of the message transmitted, in this case verbosity on the subject of brevity, and the inability to realize this incongruity on the part of the speaker. The synonymic expansion of the concept of brevity now alternates with Sganarelle's feeble attempts, however, indicating the extent to which his own language is caught up by Pancrace's. His last attempt, "Je vous . . .," summarizes the situation completely: all that has been established in this scene is the opposition of two speakers. Pancrace does not even perceive this elementary fact, as his final interruption demonstrates. Sganarelle's recourse to throwing stones at his desired listener underlines the ineffectiveness of the words he has hurled in that direction to no avail.[13]

In the scene we have been analyzing, we have observed the confrontation of two speakers who refuse to make the modifications in their language necessary to assure communication. Although both are therefore ridiculous, only one, Sganarelle, is manipulated. This situation must be explained if we are to better understand the interdependent processes of manipulation and self-betrayal. It will then remain to show how this process affects our notion of comedy. If Sganarelle's manipulation by Pancrace were completely arbitrary, that is if it were not based on some personal inadequacy of Sganarelle's, we would be tempted to be sympathetic to his plight. This sympathy on the part of the spectator would make any comic reaction impossible, as numerous theorists have demonstrated. No longer would judgments of comparison be pertinent, no longer would that affective distance essential for the comic be operative. We would have to conclude, then, that farce does not concern itself with deserved punishment, that it relies merely on an incongruity of presentation to short-circuit

---

[13] This recourse to violence where communication fails is often exploited by Molière in order to emphasize their mutual implication. Further examples of this technique will enable us to develop more fully Molière's particular formulation of this role of violence in comedy.

any affective response on the part of the spectator. This is not the case, we believe, in this play.

Sganarelle reveals his abnormal idea of language's proper use in his first appearance on stage. In this first scene, we observe him seeking out his friend Géronimo, ostensibly to ask his advice on whether he should marry. We soon realize, however, that this ostensible desire actually masks a completely different one. Let us diagram their conversation: (pp. 547–551)

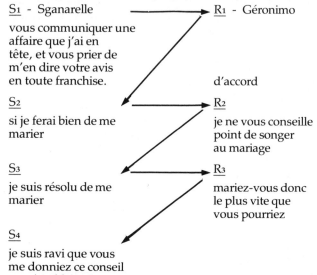

S₁ - Sganarelle → R₁ - Géronimo

vous communiquer une
affaire que j'ai en
tête, et vous prier de
m'en dire votre avis
en toute franchise.

d'accord

S₂

si je ferai bien de me
marier

R₂

je ne vous conseille
point de songer
au mariage

S₃

je suis résolu de me
marier

R₃

mariez-vous donc
le plus vite que
vous pourriez

S₄

je suis ravi que vous
me donniez ce conseil
en véritable ami.

Sganarelle's idea of "franchise" is thus limited to approval, as the sequence R₃-S₄ indicates; only when Géronimo sarcastically advises him to marry does he accept his advice. Moreover, we are forced to conclude that although Sganarelle seems to be seeking advice, he is actually seeking to justify a decision which he has already made—the contrast between S₁ and S₃ confirms this. This lip-service to honest advice so often repeated becomes all the more incongruous when we learn that

Sganarelle is certainly in need of it at this point, as Géronimo's "Vertu de ma vie" indicates. In the revelation of Sganarelle's abnormal conception of honest advice, Molière also invites us to examine his improper idea of true communication, a notion we propose to examine after a closer investigation of the motives of Sganarelle's dissimulation.[14]

Dissimulation of the type Sganarelle attempts here usually brings about manipulation of an other. This is clearly not the case, however, in this encounter. Wherein lies the weakness in Sganarelle's language, then? The nature of Sganarelle's dissimulation is obvious; his intention (I) is masked by its expression (E):

$$\frac{E \; - \; \text{give me your frank advice}}{I \; - \; \text{agree with me}}$$

Whereas another character might mask his intention in order to gather important knowledge of the other and use this knowledge against him,[15] Sganarelle is incapable of controlling his real desires:

> Et moi je vous dis que je suis résolu de me marier, et que je ne serai pas ridicule en épousant la fille que je recherche. (p. 550)

Thus Sganarelle's attempted dissimulation falls victim to his inability to keep up the appearances. The irony becomes complete with Géronimo's sarcastic approval. In summary,

---

[14] At this point, a methodological clarification is required. Our analysis of Sganarelle's utterances is based on the process of encoding, the method by which speech (expression) is formulated to communicate a particular intention. The relationship between E and I is a complex one, but one which we feel can be broken down into two general categories:

E is inappropriate for I because
    (a) it is an inadequate formulation of I
or
    (b) it is the result of a desire to dissimulate I which fails.

[15] cf. the role of Valère in *L'Avare* and his ability to manipulate Harpagon. Valère speaks one of the most powerful *positive* manipulatory languages in Molière.

then, Sganarelle speaks a curiously mixed comic language, one which he designedly misuses yet cannot fully control. While playing the "fourbe," he becomes the "fou." W. G. Moore has demonstrated the comic nature of this procedure:

> Language is as comic when designedly misused as when it unintentionally betrays. The source of comedy lies in the fact of interference in the normal process of communication; in one case the man's nature interferes with his intention; in the other his intention deliberately obscures or abandons normal speech in order to attain a particular end. [16]

Sganarelle is doubly comic therefore: not only does he fail to manipulate Géronimo, but betrays in the attempt an inability to control his own speech.

We have seen that Sganarelle's conception of language is inadequate in two basic respects: for him, communication means a search for approval of a decision already made, but not expressed, where the only response acceptable is agreement; moreover, the dissimulation he employs in this search breaks down whenever such approval is not offered. Yet why dissimulate in the first place? Why does not Sganarelle try to convince Géronimo that he is appropriate for marriage by simply stating his reasons and/or affirming the adequacy of his physical constitution?

Sganarelle's actual physical condition is difficult to discern, but it is certain that his own assessment is highly suspect. He is curiously unaware of his own age in scene one, yet admits to being "un peu avancé en âge pour elle [Dorimène]" in scene nine. Moreover, he attests in this latter scene to certain "bizarreries épouvantables" and "infirmités sur mon corps," facts which belie his judgment in scene one. Dorimène's own assessment is more in line with this later expression:

---

[16] Will G. Moore, *Molière: A New Criticism* (Garden City, 1962), p. 59.

C'est un homme qui mourra avant qu'il soit peu, et qui n'a tout au plus que six mois dans le ventre. (p. 568)

These inconsistencies indicate that we are dealing with a character who attempts to ignore reality and/or misinterpret its facts when it suits his purposes. His inability to undo this misrepresentation will be the price he must pay for this self-deception, for Alcantor is willing to accept him, "bizarreries" and all, as long as it means passing his daughter off on someone else:

Une honnête femme ne se dégoûte jamais de son mari . . . vous l'aurez en dépit de tous ceux qui y prétendent. (p. 570)

Sganarelle's actual purpose in withholding his reasons for marriage from Géronimo until it seems that the latter agrees with his plan can be deduced from two important facts concerning their transmission: the timing of their delivery and their content. It is significant that Sganarelle expressed them only after Géronimo's sarcastic

Vous avez raison; je m'étais trompé: vous ferez bien de vous marier. (p. 550)

This timing indicates a certain reticence on Sganarelle's part, betraying perhaps an uncertainty as to their appropriateness. Let us examine these reasons more closely in order to see if such an interpretation is justified.

Sganarelle appears to have two "puissantes raisons" for marriage:

Outre la joie que j'aurai de posséder une belle femme, . . . je considère que . . . je laisse périr la race des Sganarelles, et qu'en me mariant, *je pourrai me voir revivre* en d'autres moi-mêmes . . . . (p. 550)

The first of these, desire for possession, is clarified in the following scene with Dorimène:

Vous ne serez *plus en droit* de me rien refuser; et *je pourrai faire* avec vous *tout ce qu'il me plaira*, . . . Vous allez être *à moi* depuis la tête

77

> jusqu'aux pieds, et je serai maître de tout . . . toute votre per-
> sonne sera *à ma discrétion*, et je serai à même pour vous caresser
> *comme je voudrai* . . . . (pp. 552–553)

Thus for Sganarelle, marriage will be another occasion to extend his control over others, a control which he exercises through trickery.[17] The nature of this control is double, as linguistic analysis demonstrates: actively, Sganarelle considers himself capable of doing whatever he pleases—"je pourrai faire," "je serai maître," "à ma discrétion," "comme je voudrai"; passively, he considers himself the worthy object of another's attentions—"me fera mille caresses," "me dorlo-tera," "me viendra frotter." The inappropriateness of this position is manifested first of all by its inherent incongruity, but more importantly in the comparison of this "pouvoir-faire" with Dorimène's own version:

> . . . j'ai cent fois souhaité qu'il me mariât, pour sortir de la con-
> trainte où j'étais avec lui, et me voir en état de faire *ce que je voudrai*.
> (p. 553)

These words are clear enough to evoke doubt in Sganarelle for the first time, a doubt which will be the subject of the next four scenes. Thus Sganarelle has revealed by his words an ab-normal vision of himself which is in harmony neither with the facts of his own physical being nor with the situation he is in. As ridiculous as his ideas of marriage in general are to the spectator, they will become even more so in his attempt to apply them in this particular case.

Scenes three through six show us a Sganarelle complete-ly different from the self-assured character of the first two. Now suddenly uncertain, he feels the need to clarify his

---

[17] cf. his first words:
> "Si l'on m'apporte de l'argent, que l'on me
> vienne quérir vite. . . . ; si l'on vient m'en
> demander, qu'on dise que je suis sorti et
> que je ne dois revenir de toute la journée." (p. 547)

future. We have seen, however, that Sganarelle communicates solely to assure himself of a particular state of mind. The irony of each of these scenes lies in the fact that he again succeeds in getting affirmation of his position. In this case, however, it is merely the affirmation of his uncertainty. We can outline this comparison as follows:

E: pretended uncertainty $\longrightarrow$ affirmation of certainty
I: certainty

E: uncertainty $\longrightarrow$ affirmation of uncertainty
I: uncertainty

Thus, the fact that Sganarelle will add nothing to his knowledge through these scenes has actually been prepared in scenes one and two. He believes his language to be consistently "effective," but this is true only within the limits he himself has prescribed.

In the first of these scenes, scene three, Sganarelle recounts a dream he has had:

> Vous savez que les songes sont comme des miroirs, où l'on découvre quelquefois tout ce qui nous doit arriver. Il me semblait [dans ce songe] que j'étais dans un vaisseau, sur une mer bien agitée, et que . . . . (p. 554)

Although he recognizes the power of dreams in general to foretell the future[18] and is aware of the facts of his own particular dream, Sganarelle nevertheless fails to see the obvious interpretation of these facts for his own situation. This failure is due to his inability to accord a sufficient value of truth to the facts at his disposal. Moreover, it indicates that Sganarelle communicates with himself in the same way as he communicated with Géronimo: only those items which support his desires are acceptable to him. The dream in this scene func-

---

[18] For the use of this notion and its theatrical modification, cf. Corneille's "Préfaces" to *Polyeucte* and *Horace*.

tions as a type of interior "monologue" between Sganarelle's conscious and unconscious, indicating that his decisions are a result of a blind disregard of the latter's warnings. This division within his being takes the form of a self-deception which is continuously clear to the spectator, who delights in observing Sganarelle's attempts to close a gap of which he is not even aware.

In the following three scenes (sc. iv, v, vi), Sganarelle confronts three different types of characters, and therefore three different speech-systems in an attempt to clarify his future: the Aristotelian Pancrace, the pseudo-Cartesian Marphurius, and two fortune-telling Egyptians. We have already described the results of the first encounter. In the second, the discourse of Marphurius serves to exaggerate the inherent contradiction within Sganarelle's language, since Marphurius urges him to speak with uncertainty even of facts which are certain:

> Notre philosophie ordonne de ne point énoncer de proposition décisive, de parler de tout avec incertitude, de suspendre toujours son jugement; et, par cette raison, vous ne devez pas dire: "Je suis venu;" mais: "Il me semble que je suis venu." (p. 563)

That Marphurius' position is untenable is clear from Sganarelle's ability to expose its inherent contradictions in the second part of this scene simply by using Marphurius' own language on him:

> S: . . . Je viens vous dire que j'ai envie de me marier.
> M: Je n'en sais rien.
> S: Je vous le dis.
> M: Il se peut faire.
>
> . . .
> [Sganarelle lui donne des coups de bâton]
> M: C'est toi qui m'as traité ainsi.
> S: Il n'y a pas d'impossibilité.
> M: J'aurai un décret contre toi.
> S: Je n'en sais rien.
> M: Et tu seras condamné en justice.
> S: Il en sera ce qui pourra. (pp. 563, 565)

Yet this philosophy is even more comic when we apply its precepts to Sganarelle himself. Sganarelle has been guilty of a precipitous decision, one for which he consulted no one beforehand and for which he chose to disregard certain facts in the interest of self-approval. He is thus supremely worthy of manipulation at the hands of someone who is guilty of the opposite extreme, namely no deciding whatsoever and the doubting of *all* facts. The lack of communication in these encounters with philosophers is therefore not simply a gratuitous insertion unrelated to Sganarelle's linguistic inadequacies. It is rather a rigorous demonstration of the reasons for which Sganarelle's language fails to affect its supposed listener. Thus in Sganarelle's conversation with Géronimo, two consequences of his system of language were implicitly expressed: on the one hand, any supposed "conversation" that actually sought approval of an already-made judgment has no real necessity for a respondent; on the other hand, anyone who speaks with pretended uncertainty about something of which he is actually quite sure has deliberately obscured the domain of possible knowledge. It is quite fitting, then, that Sganarelle become the excluded respondent of Pancrace's discourse and that Marphurius should obscure even further Sganarelle's pretended uncertainty. This process will be completed in the scene with the Egyptians.

The language of scene six furnishes us with an excellent example of the use of a "discours à double sens" in the creation of the comic. This type of purposefully vague language, incomprehensible to Sganarelle, is however completely transparent to the spectator, who can thereby delight in Sganarelle's blindness from a position of total decoding superiority. Let us outline the main utterances of this discourse and their possible meanings:

	A	B
a) homme qui sera un jour quelque chose	important	cocu

b) femme qui sera chérie et amie de tout le monde	respected	amourous
c) qui te fera beau- coup d'amis	visitors	lovers
d) qui fera venir l'abondance	of pleasure	of misfortune
e) tu seras considéré par elle (pp. 566–567)	as a good husband	as a fool

Each register, A and B, creates an "isotopie de discours" which is at total variance to its opposite. As Greimas,[19] among others, has pointed out, it is the perception of two (or more) isotopies simultaneously presented to a spectator that is the basis of any appreciation of a "jeu de mots" or, more specifically in this case, a "double entendre." Each syntagm creates the minimal context which is supported by the global context of the passage. The process is somewhat defective in this particular example, however, since Sganarelle does not choose between the two series of possibilities, but rather is unable to decipher this language at all:

> . . . ce n'est pas là me répondre . . . Peste soit des carognes, qui me laissent dans l'inquiétude! (p. 567)

Since these statements do not express univocally what Sganarelle wants to know, he decodes nothing from expressions which actually have a *surplus* of meaning. For him, there is no such thing as poly-semantic expressions; either someone directly disagrees with him whereupon he rejects their judgment, or someone agrees with him, whereupon he accepts it. By limiting conversation in this way, Sganarelle has automatically condemned himself to the course of action he alone sees fit. Consequently, no further data, even if relevant, can be

---

[19] Algirdas J. Greimas, *Sémantique structurale* (Paris, 1966), pp. 69ff.:
"La conversation spirituelle est caractérisée par l'utilisation parallèle et successive de plusieurs isotopies à la fois."

accepted, and the words of the Egyptians reach only the spectator.

Sganarelle's powerlessness to obtain any clarification of his position contrasts strongly with Lycaste's ability to do so in scene seven. As is the case in nearly all Molière's plays, only the real lovers succeed in communicating with each other. Whereas in *George Dandin*, for example, this communication must be achieved even in the presence of the deceived husband, in farce the procedure appears much simpler: Dorimène merely declares her real intentions to Lycaste. This declaration confirms what the spectator has known from the outset, and although Sganarelle overhears it, this knowledge will be useless, for reasons we must now explain.

The entire comic moral of the play is contained in the confrontation scene between Sganarelle and Alcantor. The structure of this scene reflects perfectly the structure of scene one, but its movement is reversed: Sganarelle now judges himself from what had been Géronimo's point of view. Thus, where the first scene began with Sganarelle's repeated assurances that the marriage would take place, the spectator can almost hear Géronimo's questions behind the excuses Sganarelle now attempts:

> Géronimo à Sganarelle: Quel âge pouvez-vous avoir maintenant?
> Sganarelle à Alcantor: Je me trouve un peu avancé en âge
>   pour elle.

> Sganarelle à Géronimo: Vous semble-t-il que je ne sois plus
>   propre à songer à une femme?
> Sganarelle à Alcantor: J'ai parfois des bizarreries
>   épouvantables, et elle aurait trop à souffrir de ma
>   mauvaise humeur.

> Sganarelle à Géronimo: Y a-t-il un homme de trente ans
>   qui paraisse plus frais et plus vigoureux que vous
>   me voyez?
> Sganarelle à Alcantor: J'ai quelques infirmités sur mon
>   corps qui pourraient la dégoûter.

> Géronimo à Sganarelle: Je vous conseille de vous marier
>   le plus vite que vous pourriez.
> Sganarelle à Alcantor: Je ne vous conseille pas de me la donner.

The irony of these excuses lies in the fact that they are not Sganarelle's real reasons. In the guise of offering to spare Alcantor's daughter from an unworthy husband, Sganarelle is actually trying to avoid this "quelque chose de pis" himself. In the attempt, however, he betrays his real nature, a nature he chose to disregard when it suited his purposes. His own words sum up the total absurdity of his position:

> La raison? C'est que je ne me sens point propre pour le mariage, et que je veux imiter mon père, et tous ceux de ma race, *qui ne se sont jamais voulus marier*. (p. 571)

Assuming that Sganarelle is not illegitimate, he has expressed in these words his own future and the dénouement of the play. As the structure indicates, he *will* be able to imitate his father, but only the latter's *desire* not to marry. Sganarelle's father married against his will, and so will Sganarelle himself. The comic lies again in the total incongruity of the situation his words describe, of which Sganarelle is completely unaware.

In Alcantor's response, transmitted to Sganarelle by the former's son Alcidas, Sganarelle finally realizes the problem of a language which arbitrarily dissimulates its speaker's desires. Words which dissimulate unfortunately remain convincing. Their power to convince can be more a function of what a listener chooses to believe for his own reasons than of how well these words hide the desires of their speaker. Most Molière "fourbes" are capable of adjusting these two aspects, personal desire and the beliefs another is susceptible to, in a way which reconciles the two where and when it suits their purposes. In our analysis, however, Sganarelle reveals himself as a poor manipulator. Thus, his attempt in scene eight to give a new interpretation to facts he has chosen to misrepresent fails before Alcantor's own choice to disregard them. The latter, then, is the real winner:

Loué soit le Ciel! M'en voilà déchargé, et c'est vous desormais que regarde le soin de sa conduite. (p. 574)

Our analysis of *Le Mariage forcé* has permitted us to test our basic hypothesis that Molière's theater is concerned with the use and misuse of language. This concern is manifested on two interdependent levels: through his linguistic formulations, the Molière character attempts to manipulate reality in a way that will assure manipulation of his listener and guarantee the satisfaction of his own desires; this manipulation is dangerous, however, for it exposes its user to the whims of the one he attempts to control and presents the incongruity of his expressions to the spectator. In farce, it appears that this manipulation, and, where it fails, self-betrayal, proceed along rather rudimentary lines. Failure to respect the elementary rules of communication is at the basis of Sganarelle's and Pancrace's inadequate powers of language; simple refusal to believe Sganarelle's self-deprecations is the secret of Alcantor's successful manipulation. Nowhere is it a question of desires of profound social importance; rather, all the characters of the play betray certain personal conceptions of reality which are ridiculous more in their presentation than in any inherent inadequacy. Moreover, the spectator remains supremely aware of the games each character plays with language. Thus, rather than justifying the arbitrary interpretation of reality he would impose on others, Sganarelle's incompetent manipulation reveals its illogicalness and contradiction.

The general application of these insights to farce and to the more subtle comedies remains to be tested. One idea seems particularly promising, however: the pre-requisite for all successful manipulation is an awareness on the part of the pretended manipulator of the arbitrariness of his formulations. Without it, he is incapable of comprehending the person he attempts to convince, but more importantly, he exposes himself to the discrepancies in his own thought and becomes their slave. Sganarelle measured up poorly to this requirement, being unaware of his ridiculousness even when directly laughed at:

> Ce mariage doit être heureux, car il donne de la joie à tout le monde, et je fais rire tous ceux à qui j'en parle. Me voilà maintenant le plus content des hommes. (p. 552)

Finally, through this demonstration of complementarily inadequate speech systems, Molière succeeds in giving this play an internal coherence and a message about language's correct use. The pretended manipulator, Sganarelle, finds himself thwarted by characters whose language strategies unconsciously reflect his own misuse of language. More importantly, however, Molière raises important linguistic questions—the relationships of thought and language, language and truth—which indicate that he was supremely aware of his century's preoccupations. In ridiculing Pancrace, Molière questions the value of the optimistic theory which would hold that language perfectly reflects thought. While this may be true, and it must be if Molière's theater is to avoid total problematicity, it is not sufficient, since it does not take into account the modifications in language necessary for communication with a specific respondent. On the other hand, by enabling even Sganarelle to defeat Marphurius, Molière questions the skeptic's position on language as well. Whereas language may be in effect as uncertain as referential reality, a point we will investigate in *le Cocu imaginaire*, in language as in reality there are certain undeniable truths. The "correct" use of language, then, would be one in which language is modified for the given circumstances and is founded on solid evidence.

VII.   Sganarelle ou le Cocu imaginaire

Sganarelle, ou le Cocu imaginaire is, at first glance, a farce that does not seem to concern itself with the use and misuse of language. Its plot develops from one important misjudgment by Sganarelle's wife which creates a series of situational qui-proquo's that gradually reach all four main characters. As a result, by scene xxiii, each has developed his own interpretation of the relationships between the other three. Because of the complex nature of this process, we propose to study this farce from a different direction. Beginning with the resulting misunderstandings, we will attempt to investigate the reasons thereof, gradually retracing the sequence of misconceptions to their source in the language systems of each character. Let us begin then by summarizing the situation reached in scene xxii:

		his wife		Lélie's lover
Sganarelle	believes ←	Lélie	is ←	his wife's lover
		Célie		someone who supports his desire for revenge

		Sganarelle		Célie's lover
his wife	believes ←	Lélie	is ←	someone she has helped
		Célie		Sganarelle's lover

```
                    Sganarelle's wife          someone who helped him
Lélie    believes ←Sganarelle            is ←Célie's husband
                    Célie                      Sganarelle's wife

                    Sganarelle's wife          Lélie's lover
Célie    believes ←Sganarelle            is ←the deceived husband
                    Lélie                      Sganarelle's wife's lover
```

The original misunderstanding between Sganarelle and his wife is based on the misperception of a reality which is clearly presented to the spectator. While not related directly to linguistic (i.e. grammatical) incompetence, the character traits which have made this misperception possible are nevertheless revealed through the use each makes of language. In scene four, we observe Sganarelle examining Célie who has fainted:

> Elle est froide partout et je ne sais qu'en dire
> *Approchons-nous* pour voir si sa bouche respire. (p. 228)

His wife interprets this action as infidelity:

> Ah! qu'est-ce que je voi?
> Mon mari *dans ses bras*! . . . (p. 228)

Similarly, when Sganarelle sees his wife examining the portrait of Lélie that Célie has dropped, he mistakenly perceives her action of smelling it as kissing:

> Femme: Jamais rien de plus beau ne s'offrît à ma vue.
>   Le travail plus que l'or s'en doit encore priser.
>   Ho! que cela *sent* bon!
> Sganarelle: Quoi? peste! le *baiser*! (pp. 229–230)

These misperceptions are not presented gratuitously, however, for both Sganarelle and his wife betray the type of suspicious mind necessary for such judgments of reality. Both, it seems, seize on this particular pretext to confront the other with proof of infidelity. This accusation has probably been the principal topic of discussion since the beginning of their marriage. Sganarelle chooses to interpret the action as he does because this can explain his wife's disregard for him:

> Donc, à votre calcul, ô ma trop digne femme,
> Monsieur, tout bien compté, ne vaut pas bien Madame? (p. 230)

whereas his wife chooses to believe she has found the reasons
for his lack of attention toward her:

> Je ne m'étonne plus de l'étrange froideur
> Dont je le vois répondre à ma pudique ardeur:
> Il réserve, l'ingrat, ses caresses à d'autres,
> Et nourrit leur plaisir par le jeûne des nôtres. (p. 229)

Thus their misjudgments are the result of a desire to see things
in the way they choose and not simple misunderstandings
rectifiable by seeking further information. Molière touches
here a fundamental problem of perception: *the interference of
desire in the evaluation of observed situations*. In *Tartuffe*, the *facts*
of Tartuffe's actions will be agreed on by all and it will be their
interpretation that causes disagreement. For Sganarelle and his
wife, the problem is much more basic: it is the facts themselves
that are wrongly perceived. Moreover, where the spectator
would expect them to afford each other the opportunity to
explain, he finds rather that each seeks an explanation *within
himself*:

> F: Ah! Qu'est-ce que je vois?
>
> . . . . .
>   Il me trahit sans doute. (p. 228)
> S: Que considère-t-elle avec attention?
>
> . . . . .
>   Ce portrait, mon honneur, ne nous dit rien de bon.
>   D'un fort vilain soupçon je me sens l'âme émue.
>   (p. 229)

The conversation that takes place between two characters
whose judgments are thus formulated can only be a confrontation between self-motivated assertions where proof is the
starting point rather than the ultimate aim:

> S: La chose est *avérée* et je tiens dans mes mains
>   Un bon certificat du mal dont je me plains. (p. 230)
> F: Donc, *après m'avoir fait* la plus sensible offense. . .
>   (p. 231)

Piaget has demonstrated the existence of such quarreling between children aged 4 to 7:

> We may distinguish two stages of childish argument. The first consists in a simple clash of contrary tendencies and opinions. This gives us two more or less contemporaneous types—the primitive quarrel and the primitive argument. The second consists in arguments in which the speakers give the *motives* of their respective points of view.[20]

The comic here is double, it seems: in the first place, the opinions expressed are not founded on abstractions but rather on the incorrect perception of factual data; secondly, the spectator is aware, unlike the characters, of the motives for such behavior. The two isotopies here observed by the spectator are in fundamental opposition: Sganarelle and his wife are actually arguing opinions, whereas the spectator observes this clash from a correct perception of factual data. We will examine this superior position subsequently in the context of the entire play.

It is exactly this desire to confront the other with supposed proof, rather than to discuss circumstances, which enables the series of misunderstandings to continue. In light of this, the fact that Sganarelle and his wife do not "converse" further until scene xxii becomes more than a simple theatrical exigency for the continuation of the plot. Rather, it is the direct consequence of their shared belief that no conversation is necessary or possible.

Whereas Sganarelle and his wife have been presented with an ambiguous *situation* which each misinterprets, Lélie and Célie have only Sganarelle's words on which to base any judgments. The former sees Sganarelle with his portrait and asks where he got it. Sganarelle, recognizing Lélie from the portrait, responds:

---

[20] Piaget, pp. 83ff.

S: Il était en des mains *de votre connaissance*.
   Et ce n'est pas un fait qui soit secret pour nous
   Que les douces ardeurs de la dame et de vous.

L: Quoi! celle, dites-vous, qui *conservait* ce gage. . .

S: Est ma femme, et je suis son mari. (p. 235)

Whereupon Lélie immediately forgets (?) the faith he protested in Célie,[21] concluding:

On me l'avait bien dit, et que c'était de tous
L'homme le plus mal fait qu'elle avait pour époux. (p. 235)[22]

The process is similar for Célie: having seen Sganarelle with Lélie, she asks the former how he knows him:

Ce damoiseau, parlant par révérence,
Me fait cocu, Madame, avec toute licence;
Et j'ai su *par mes yeux* avérer aujourd'hui
Le commerce secret de ma femme et de lui. (p. 238)

Whereupon Célie immediately forgets (?) the faith *she* protested in Lélie,[23] concluding:

Ah! j'avais bien jugé que ce secret retour
Ne pouvait me couvrir que quelque lâche tour;
Et j'ai tremblé d'abord, en le voyant paraître,
Par un pressentiment de ce qui devait être. (p. 238)

These two judgments, Lélie's "on me l'avait bien dit" and Célie's "J'avais bien jugé," indicate the shallowness of the faith each protested in the other, a faith which gives way before the desire for self-righteousness. Once this shallowness is betrayed by their reactions to the first situations which would cast any doubt on this faith, the spectator realizes that there is little difference between this couple and the other. Again, we are observing two suspicious minds which seize upon a simple circumstance, Sganarelle's words, as an ex-

---

[21] cf. p. 233, vv. 250–252.

[22] It never occurs to Lélie that there would be no reason whatsoever for Célie to give *his* portrait to *her* new "husband."

[23] cf. p. 227, vv. 98–102.

planation of what they expected to happen, Lélie to explain "ce funeste bruit," Célie "ce secret retour."

Thus in this curious farce where no character attempts to manipulate another, the spectator observes rather an impersonal manipulatory force. For the couple Sganarelle-wife, it is the force of "appearances" which can function, however, only when nourished by the desire to see in these appearances a confirmation of their own suspicions. For the couple Célie-Lélie, it is also the force of appearances, joined in this case with an unwarranted faith in an other's interpretation of misperceived reality and made possible by pre-existent suspicions. Four characters, then, who allow themselves to be manipulated yet betray quite clearly that they are susceptible to, and therefore worthy of, this manipulation.

The position of the spectator in this play is one of rudimentary superiority; he has all the facts at his disposal whereas the characters he observes do not. This farce of coherent reasoning based on false perceptions is, despite its complex plot, one of the easiest to follow, as Judd Hubert has remarked:

> The spectator derives his greatest pleasure from following *with the utmost clarity* the ever-increasing aberrations of the characters involved.[24]

More than simply inviting the spectator to observe reason gone wild, however, Molière has again presented a fundamental aspect of the problematic of language—that language's veracity is a function of the desired beliefs of a listener and, therefore, that it escapes the control of its speaker. Two observations, however, will show that in this particular farce, this problematic is posed in rather simple terms.

First of all, unlike in *Le Mariage forcé*, no character seeks to control his language in order to manipulate another. This fact

---

[24] Judd D. Hubert, *Molière and the Comedy of Intellect* (Los Angeles, 1962), p. 25.

is based on the belief that no such control is necessary, imply-
ing a blind acceptance of language's ability to represent reality.
It is this blind acceptance that Molière was actually ridiculing,
we believe, proposing by implication a procedure that would
be based on interrogation of sources and re-examination of
circumstantial evidence. In presenting the difference between
actual reality and its misperception effected by the intervention of the suspicious imagination, Molière has demonstrated
the consequent aberrations of a language cut off from the
ultimate justification of its adequacy, its referent. Let us
attempt to outline this system. In general:

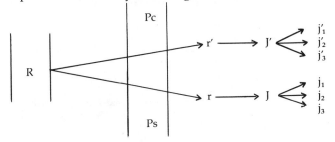

where the reference (R) is perceived by a character (Pc) and by
the spectator (Ps). In the first case, a mistaken response (r')
based on Pc generates a mistaken judgment (J') which entails
various incorrect conclusions (j'$_1$, etc.). In the second case, a
correct response (r) based on the spectator's superior percep-
tive position (Ps) generates a correct judgment (J) which entails
various correct conclusions (j$_1$, etc.). For Sganarelle, then:

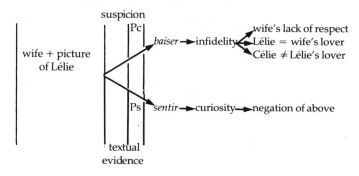

Or for Sganarelle's wife:

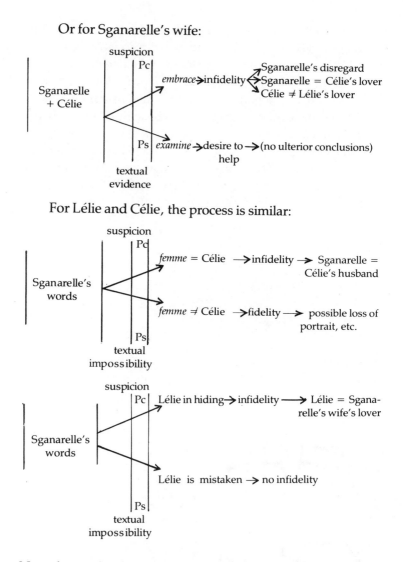

For Lélie and Célie, the process is similar:

Note that in this farce, the problem occurs in the denotation of the referent. In more sophisticated comedies, this problem will shift to its connotation(s), since the *facts* of the behavior observed will not be disputed:

94

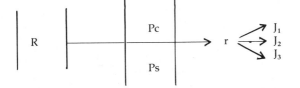

In this farce, then, the spectator's superior factual perception removes the threat of misinterpretation for him, whereas in comedies where $Pc = Ps$, this superiority must be based on an ability to discredit the *judgments* of the misled characters.

The second factor which leads us to believe that Molière has presented a simplified version of language's misuse is based on the relative insufficient evidence of character motivation. Hubert has outlined this weakness as follows:

> Whereas in later comedies, Molière will endeavor to establish causal connections between internal and external contradictions [for his characters], in *Sganarelle*, he is quite content to associate them by means of analogy or even juxtaposition.[25]

We have shown that the internal contradictions in this play are joined to their external counterparts by the existence of the same fault of perception, generated by mistrust, in all four characters. In terms of a moral of language, Molière has demonstrated how this misperception of reality can give rise to a "false" language which can nevertheless become the basis for further misperception. Implicit to this demonstration is the affirmation that both language and referential reality must be judged with the utmost circumspection.

---

[25] Hubert, p. 26.

VIII.   Le Médecin volant

Le Médecin volant and La Jalousie du Barbouillé were Molière's first attempts at farce and as such present important material for a study of the origins and rudiments of his future comic situations. Though their authorship is often questioned, we believe that the three-act comedies into which they were developed, Le Médecin malgré lui and George Dandin, show enough evidence of a similar style and treatment that these farces be considered an integral part of Molière's comic theater.

Sganarelle of Le Médecin volant presents us with the first wilful manipulator of language in Molière. Although this play is ostensibly concerned with the victory of two lovers over an avaricious father, it is clearly Sganarelle who occupies our attention. The play's three major aspects all center on his actions: the self-betrayal of Gorgibus, the manipulation of Sganarelle by Valère, and Sganarelle's manipulation of Gorgibus, including success, discovery, and ultimate triumph.

Scene one introduces Gorgibus to the spectator through the words of Sabine. Although this introduction is rather cursory, we are given to observe two important aspects of his character, his avarice and his credulity. Sabine informs us that his proposed marriage for his daughter Lucile was conceived "par l'avarice de mon vilain oncle" (p. 23). Gorgibus himself reinforces this characteristic in scene three, wherein it becomes clear that he is more interested in curing his daughter because of the delay her "illness" is causing, rather than through any paternal anxiety for her health:

> Va-t'en vite; je vois bien que cette maladie-là reculera bien les noces. (p. 25)

In this attitude, he prefigures the Gorgibus of *Le Cocu imaginaire*, and other "père-bourgeois" who manifest these obsessions in much greater depth. Sabine, however, insists on this father's credulity, ("Il n'y a rien de si facile à duper que le bonhomme"), and proves her point by revealing his ready belief in Lucile's illness:

> C'est que ma cousine. . .contrefait la malade; et le bon vieillard, qui est asez crédule, m'envoie quérir un médecin. (p. 23)

This "bonne invention" requires further development, however, namely a doctor who will go along with the game. Valère agrees on Sganarelle, his valet, simply since he has no other choice: ". . .il faut s'en servir faute d'autre" (p. 23).

Scene two presents a classic example of how to use language to manipulate another into doing something he would prefer not to. As such, it presents an interesting comparison with scene one of *Le Mariage forcé*. Valère has already indicated his feelings toward Sganarelle to the spectator ("C'est un lourdaud qui gâtera tout!"), but of course does not reveal them to Sganarelle himself. Let us outline and summarize the development of this scene:

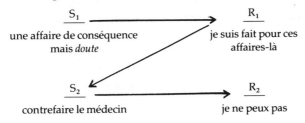

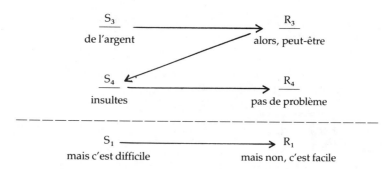

Valère's expression of doubt in Sganarelle's ability scores the first gain in this conversation: he has wounded Sganarelle's self-image as an "habile homme" who believes in his ability to accomplish important tasks. This ability does not extend to playing a doctor, however, but Valère shores up Sganarelle's confidence with the offer of payment. When this does not completely succeed, Valère resorts to insults, but rather curiously polite ones. He does not betray his firm belief that Sganarelle will definitely ruin things—the previous use of the future "gâtera"—but simply indicates a slight suspicion that this could be the outcome—the conditional "pourrais." Sganarelle, seeing the prospect of payment slipping through his fingers, hastens to affirm his ability and accepts. Valère has him now, delivering the clinching argument that "Il n'y a rien de si facile en cette rencontre," and furnishes Sganarelle with the tools he will need:

> Gorgibus . . . se laissera étourdir de ton discours, pourvu que tu parles d'Hippocrate et de Galien, et que tu sois un peu effronté. (pp. 24–25)

In these words, Valère summarizes the aspects of a well-controlled, manipulatory language: a willing dupe, a vocabulary whose form compensates for its lack of substance, and a speaker with confidence. It is interesting to note that Valère reveals this technique to Sganarelle even as he uses it on him. Sganarelle realizes, however, that his possibility for success is directly proportional to Gorgibus' weakness:

. . . s'il est un homme facile comme vous le dites, je vous réponds de tout. (p. 25)

In scene four, Sganarelle pursues his task with some difficulty, using his language well to manipulate Gorgibus yet being forced to save himself adroitly when the actual weakness of this language threatens to betray him. This scene develops through alternation of these two movements, with Sganarelle holding tenaciously to the precarious balance between manipulation and self-betrayal. Citing Hippocrates and Galien as he was instructed, Sganarelle's first discourse presents a tautology in the form of deduction:

Galien . . . persaude qu'une personne ne se porte pas bien quand elle est malade. (p. 26)

These words owe their veracity, then, to their deductive *form* and their presentation as a citation from a well-known doctor, two factors which can impress Gorgibus. Moreover, their efficacity indicates the delicate difference between deceiver and deceived, for Sganarelle and Gorgibus are equal in their knowledge of medicine: Sganarelle's success is clearly in his presentation, and not because of any superior knowledge. The valet-doctor continues to impress his dupe with an absurd mixture of Arabic, French, Italian and Latin:

Salamalec, salamalec. Rodrigue, as-tu du *coeur*? Signor, si; signor, non. Per omnia saecula saeculorum. (p. 26)

In all but the French, Sganarelle is on safe ground: Gorgibus comprehends nothing of this babbling. The French is justified by the use of *coeur* which, in the mouth of a doctor, can easily be understood by Gorgibus as an organ of the body, not a metaphor for courage. At this point, Sganarelle forgets himself and proceeds to take the father's pulse. Sabine corrects him, but it is the valet who saves himself:

. . . le sang du père et de la fille ne sont qu'une chose, et par l'altération de celui du père, je puis connaître la maladie de la fille . . . . (p. 26)

Again, an explanation whose efficacity is based on purely formal effect: its presentation as an undeniable fact of logic.[26] The game continues with Sganarelle drinking the urine of his patient (which is really white wine) and explaining this action as a sort of physical experimentation which distinguishes him from the ordinary doctor.

Scene five opens with another tautology, this time in the form of conclusive reasoning. Here Sganarelle supports his previous tautologies by introducing a "middle term" drawn from "experience," namely questioning the patient:

> S: Vous êtes malade?
> L: Oui, Monsieur.
> S: Tant pis! c'est une marque que vous ne vous portez pas bien. (p. 27)

Sganarelle slips while citing Ovid as a great doctor—fortunately Gorgibus has never heard of him—but recovers again with a dazzling series of tautologies, which we will summarize:

connexité	$\longrightarrow$	rapport
mélancholie	=	ennemi de la joie
bile	=	ce qui rend jaune
la maladie	=	contraire à la santé

$\therefore$ votre fille est malade

Again, the conclusion of this "syllogism" is in no way related to the sequential deduction of truth from propositions, but rather owes its effect to a sort of demonstration by contagion: it is presented at the end of a series of incontrovertible metalinguistic statements. The only resemblance to logical deduction is the purely linear presentation of propositions joined by the

---

[26] Note also that Sganarelle ironically reveals his awareness of what has caused Lucile's illness, namely her father's choice of a wealthy suitor over Valère. This is the actual "altération" to which Sganarelle alludes.

important words *comme, car,* and *nous pouvons dire.* For Gorgibus, this is more than sufficient, however, since he is interested in results at any price. Sganarelle's final slip occurs when he accidentally admits that he does not know how to write, but this he quickly "corrects":

> Ah! je ne m'en souvenais pas; j'ai tant d'affaires dans la tête, que j'oublie la moitié. (p. 28)

Gorgibus is so well manipulated linguistically by Sganarelle that he himself proposes exactly what Valère and Sabine had wished—to let his daughter have access to the garden where she and Valère can meet.

At this point in the action, Sganarelle's power has indeed become awesome. Molière demonstrates this increase in scene eight where Sganarelle disposes of a truly intelligent lawyer in one short sentence of meaningless "latin." As with Pancrace, this lawyer's statements are sound and appropriate:

> Tous les propos de l'avocat sont remarquablement sensés; ils contiennent un éloge fort juste de la médecine et une conscience claire de ses difficultés.[27]

Yet Sganarelle's one senseless line is worth all this lawyer's knowledge as far as Gorgibus is concerned. With this last victory, however, Sganarelle's linguistic manipulation is finished. From here on, he will be forced to manipulate reality in order to keep hidden the fact that he has deceived Gorgibus. It is Sganarelle who is in danger now, and only the most adroit control of appearances will save him.

In the five following scenes, Sganarelle succeeds in convincing Gorgibus that he is really two characters, doctor and valet, even to the point where Gorgibus believes he *sees* both. Though no longer manipulating linguistically, it is this previous success which spurs him on:

> Puisque j'ai tant fait, poussons la fourbe jusqu'au bout. (p. 33)

---

[27] *Molière: Oeuvres complètes,* vol. I, note 47, p. 881.

This action accelerates greatly, with Sganarelle "flying" from window to window, changing from valet to doctor and back as a concretization of his double language, while Gorgibus plods along from door to door seeking the reconciliation of two characters who are really one. Deceiver and deceived seem connected by invisible strings pulling each in different directions:

> (Pendant que Gorgibus *entre* dans la maison par la porte, Sganarelle y *entre* par la fenêtre).
> (Gorgibus *sort* de la maison par la porte et Sganarelle par la fenêtre). (pp. 33–34)

This movement reaches its climax when Gorgibus, at Gros-René's advice, demands to see both "twins" embrace. Sganarelle is equal to the task, however:

> (Il embrasse son chapeau et sa fraise, qu'il a mis au bout de son coude). (p. 35)

The position of the spectator throughout these actions is again one of rudimentary superiority—he knows from the outset that Sganarelle is not two characters. While he clearly admires Sganarelle's adroitness, his laughter is most surely directed against Gorgibus' credulity. This farce is one of Molière's gayest, since the spectator is in no way threatened by any characters, nor are the characters themselves threatened by each other. Nor does Molière let the game escape the controlling power of the theater itself, as will be the case in *Tartuffe* and *Dom Juan*, where outside intervention will be necessary to conclude the action. Rather, Sganarelle's deception is uncovered by Gros-René not because of any mistake Sganarelle could have prevented, but because the deception was no longer realistically possible to continue. Thus, although Molière has given his deceiver tremendous powers, he realizes that these powers must be limited. Sganarelle has entered a domain, reality, which must not be tampered with arbitrarily.

Yet at the same time, if Sganarelle has merited discovery, he has not merited punishment for, after all, the purpose of his deception was to restore the natural order of things. This he explains to Gorgibus in scene xv:

> Il est vrai que c'est par mon invention que mon maître est avec votre fille; mais en le servant, je ne vous ai point désobligé: c'est un parti sortable pour elle, tant pour la naissance que pour les biens. Croyez-moi, ne faites point un vacarme qui tournerait à votre confusion, et envoyez à tous les diables ce coquin-là [Gros-René], avec Villebrequin. (p. 36)

His salvation, then, is not due, as some would have it, to the pure gratuitousness of farce, but rather to a combination of factors: his adroitness and the goodness of his intentions. This is the meaning of Gorgibus' "fortunate deception":

> Je vous pardonne, et suis *heureusement trompé* par Sganarelle, ayant un si brave gendre. (p. 36)

Structurally speaking, then, this farce actually consists of two distinct scenarios: Sganarelle's discursive manipulation which necessitates his manipulation of appearances. Molière has again presented two types of referents, words and appearances, which are misinterpreted by Gorgibus. Let us outline these two procedures:

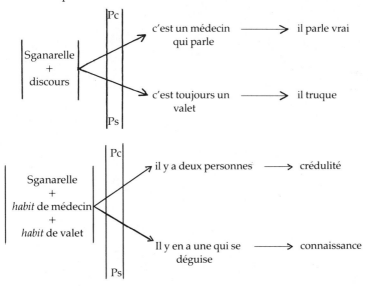

103

Thus Gorgibus' fundamental problem of perception, namely the belief that two different outfits necessarily mean two different characters, is reflected on the level of linguistic comprehension by the belief that one discourse necessarily means one person. This simplistic notion implies that for Gorgibus, words and outfits are unmistakable signs: only a doctor speaks as a doctor, only a doctor dresses like a doctor. On the other hand, the spectator is aware throughout that this notion falls apart where dissimulation is added. The comic moral of the play lies in the comparison between these two notions, for the spectator realizes that a change of language is just as likely to mislead as a change of outfit. Yet Molière underlines one important difference between manipulation by words and manipulation by objects: the former process is much surer since its weaknesses can only be uncovered by a superior intelligence. Manipulation by objects sooner or later is confronted by the objects themselves. Again we see that farce opts for a demonstration of this absolute comparison, words vs. objects, rather than for the more subtle comparison between connotations of the same denotative referent.

IX. La Jalousie du Barbouillé

La Jalousie du Barbouillé is, like *Le Cocu imaginaire*, a farce where no conscious linguistic manipulation occurs. Accordingly, no true resolution of the play's action is reached; the spectator is invited to assume that this marital game "Qui sera le plus habile?" will begin again the next day with the same evidence, the same tricks, and the same "result." As with Sganarelle in *Le Mariage forcé*, Barbouillé attempts to prove something; in the first case, the mistakenness of a decision, in the second, his own dishonor. The two plays form, with *Le Mariage forcé*, an interesting commentary on three successive states: doubt, suspicion, and actual proof.

The play itself presents three principle characters and their languages, Barbouillé, Barbouillé's wife, and a doctor. In scene one, Barbouillé defines the terms of the conflict between him and his wife:

> Il faut pourtant la punir. Si tu la tuais? . . . L'invention ne vaut rien, car tu serais pendu. Si tu la faisais mettre en prison? . . .La carogne en sortirait avec son passe-partout. (p. 7)

Unlike the situation in *George Dandin*, this conflict implicates neither society nor morality; Barbouillé rejects murder, since it will do him no good if he is hung afterwards, and prison, since he is sure it will not be effective. Thus the main conflict of the play centers not around truth or the suspicion of truth, but rather around the means to punish. Thus it will be resolved by the adroit manipulation of facts. Barbouillé's monologue introduces the spectator to the adversaries and gives indications of their relative powers and weaknesses: Barbouillé is the typical jealous husband who cannot control his wife, who appears more adroit in her ability to circumvent her husband's desires. From the outset, however, neither seems particularly threatening to the spectator, who remains aware of his own superiority to all the play's characters.

In scene two, Barbouillé attempts to communicate his problem to a "docteur." This scene presents numerous examples of comic effects arising from the difference between two linguistic systems and the recognition by the spectator that both are inferior to his own. Thus, whereas both the doctor and Barbouillé may seem ridiculous to each other, both are equally ridiculous to the spectator, whose judgment is thus directed against: (i) the doctor's timing in presenting a particular idea, (ii) the correctness of this idea, and (iii) Barbouillé's inability to redirect the discussion, evidenced by inappropriate responses. It seems that Molière has added an extra dimension to the comic use of language: whereas Pancrace's utterances in *Le Mariage forcé* were correctly formulated and became ridiculous only because mal à propos, the doctor's language in this play is patently inaccurate, as well as non-sequential to the topic of conversation. Thus two important aspects of the latter's language must be analyzed, its non-relationship to the stimuli which provoke it and its illogicality, in order to determine its absurdity. This analysis raises the question of Barbouillé's inability to manipulate these inadequacies, a question which finds its response in the inadequacies of his own language.

106

Barbouillé's first statement of his problem fails to reach his desired listener because it has not been prefaced by the correct laudatory salutation:

> . . . tu m'abordes sans ôter ton chapeau. . .Quoi! débuter. . .par un discours mal digéré, au lieu de dire: 'Salve, vel Salvus sis, Doctor, Doctorium eruditissime'. (p. 7)

His attempt to remedy this indiscretion causes him even further difficulty, however:

> B: . . .je sais bien que vous êtes galant homme.
> D: Sais-tu bien d'où vient *le mot de* galant homme?
> B: Qu'il vienne de Villejuif ou d'Aubervilliers, je ne m'en soucie guère.
> D: Sache que le mot de galant homme vient d'élégant, prenant le G et l'A de la dernière syllabe, cela fait GA, et puis prenant L, ajoutant un A et les deux dernières lettres, cela fait GALANT, et puis ajoutant HOMME, cela fait GALANT HOMME. . . (pp. 7–8)

In this particular series of rejoinders, the key to the malentendu is the expression "d'où vient," which is polysemantic. For Barbouillé, it evokes the image of geographic origins, while for the doctor it evokes the "intellectual" idea of derivation. The exclusive use each makes of the expression serves to indicate the particular isotopie of meaning each is concerned with: for Barbouillé, the realm of physical data; for the doctor, the realm of abstract concepts. The spectator is of course aware of both and consequently finds both speakers ridiculous, since neither is aware of the other's concerns. The doctor is particularly ridiculous here, since he continues his explanation even after Barbouillé has expressed his disinterest.

The doctor's language, however, goes beyond simple absurd inappropriateness to betray even deeper inadequacies. Not only must we conclude that conversational stimuli of the type "vous êtes galant homme" evoke a desire to explain the form of its expression rather than to respond to its meaning, but more importantly, this explanation is wholly preposterous. To derive GALANT HOMME from ELEGANT requires the belief that words are somehow related by the letters they share.[28] This process reminds us of Cratyle's belief that the letter T contained in both ASTYANAX and HECTOR is a justification of their sharing the same qualities of strength and courage.[29] By manipulating the graphic form of an expression then, the doctor believes he can explain its etymology. This ridiculous idea indicates a fundamental misunderstanding of the linguistic concept of arbitrary sign-creation, for although both "galant" and "élégant" were originally arbitrarily linked to the concepts their antecedents expressed (OF galer = s'amuser; L elegans = grâce), this arbitrariness cannot be extended to their etymological connections. This same process is at work in scene six, where "bonnet" is derived from "bonum est." In this case, however, the doctor proposes a relationship of similar effect:

> Cela [bonnet] vient de "bonum est" (bon est, voilà qui est bon) parce qu'il garantit des catarrhes et fluxions. (p. 13)

These mental gymnastics are as ridiculous to Barbouillé as the latter's simplicity is to the doctor. Both languages are ridiculous to the spectator, however, who can see the speciousness of the proposed etymologies at the same time as he appreciates Barbouillé's inability to avoid provoking such inappropriate responses.

Barbouillé's persistence is answered in a similarly digressive fashion:

> B: Je vous prends pour *un* docteur. . .
> D: Sache auparavant que je ne suis
> pas seulement *un* docteur, mais
> que je suis une, deux, trois,
> quatre, cinq, six, sept, huit,
> neuf et dix fois docteur. . . . (p. 8)

---

[28] Note that this "etymology" is in no way phonetic, but graphic.
[29] *Cratyle*, Plato.

Again the misunderstanding lies in the polysemanticity of "un," Barbouillé intending the indefinite article, the doctor the first element of a series. The ten reasons proposed by the doctor divide themselves into two types: those where a number is joined to an abstract concept:

$$1 = \text{unité}$$
$$3 = \text{perfection}$$
$$6 = \text{travail}$$
$$7 = \text{félicité}$$
$$8 = \text{justice}$$

and those where a number is related to a certain discipline of the same amount of parts:

2 = facultés pour la parfaite connaissance: sens, entendement
4 = parties de la philosophie: logique, morale,
      physique, métaphysique
5 = universelles: genre, espèce, différence,
      propre, accident
9 = Muses

For the first type, the syllogism is as follows:

$$\text{number(x)} = \text{qualité(y)}$$
$$\text{je possède cette qualité (y)}$$

$$\therefore \quad \text{je suis x fois docteur}$$

Its falsity is based on a fundamental misinterpretation, however: the number involved is translated into a multiplication of "doctorness" by means of a middle term, "qualité," whose relationship to the number is *totally* arbitrary. Therefore, since no factual evidence is introduced at any point, the laws of logic demand that the conclusion reached be as arbitrary as the premise. Moreover, this conclusion is incorrect; a true deduction would be:

$$3 = \text{perfection}$$
$$\text{je suis parfait}$$

$$\therefore \quad \text{je suis 3 (le chiffre)}$$

For the second type, the logic is just slightly less ridiculous:

$$\frac{\text{number}(x) = \text{number}(x): \text{parts of discipline}(y)}{\text{je possède cette discipline}}$$

$$\therefore \quad \text{je suis } x \text{ fois docteur}$$

again since the number x is transformed into a multiplication of "doctorness."

In scene six, the doctor continues his technique of turning all language toward a pseudo-consecration of his personal qualities. This technique is again two-fold: either he turns aside all language not related to these qualities or he responds only to those parts which pertain to them. Thus when it seems that Gorgibus will finally be able to communicate the actual problem to him, the doctor manages to exasperate him with six verbose pronouncements on the virtue of brevity. Or again, when Villebrequin makes the same attempt, he reproaches him for not prefacing his remarks with the appropriate "exordium." On the other hand, even though Barbouillé's "Monsieur le Docteur" reaches him, this is only because it reminds him of his greatness:

> Voilà qui est bien commencé; 'Monsieur le Docteur!' Ce mot de "Docteur" a quelque chose de doux à l'oreille, quelque chose pleine d'emphase: 'Monsieur le Docteur'. (p. 15)

We have been dealing so far primarily with the doctor's manipulation and denial of the words of others, a manipulation so complete that it destroys all communication. Yet the doctor has betrayed in the process several inherent weaknesses, namely ignorance and pretentiousness. Why cannot Barbouillé exploit these weaknesses for his own profit? The answer lies in how much Barbouillé has comprehended through all this babble. It is clear that he has in no way followed the doctor's ten-fold fallacious reasoning in scene two, and therefore would find it impossible either to accept or reject. All he has heard are the numbers:

> . . . .je trouve un ramoneur de cheminée qui, au lieu de me parler, s'amuse à jouer à la mourre. (p. 9)

110

Nor has he understood the real meaning of the doctor's seeming refusal of payment. This "refusal," too lengthy to cite here, furnishes us with an excellent example of a double self-betrayal: on the part of the doctor whose hyper-attention to details negates his ostensible propos of denying payment, and on the part of Barbouillé who is unable to understand that anyone who can so vividly describe money while refusing it is actually indicating how greatly he desires it. Thus his reaction to this speech betrays a complete inability to speak the "language" of the other:

> Ma foi, je m'y suis surpris: à cause qu'il est vêtu comme un médecin, j'ai cru qu'il lui fallait parler de l'argent; mais puisqu'il n'en veut point, il n'y a rien de plus aisé que de le contenter. (p. 10)

This inability is nowhere more clearly indicated than at the end of scene six:

> D: "Audi, quaeso," aurait dit Ciceron [sisərɔ̃]
> B: Oh! ma foi si se rompt [sisərɔ̃],
> si se casse, ou si se brise, je
> ne m'en mets guère en peine. . . (p. 15)

By this response, Barbouillé indicates a deficiency in his power to reformulate the phonic impressions he receives into their transmitted form. This inability requires us to assume that the series of phonemes corresponds to only one semantic "découpage" for Barbouillé, "si se rompt," and that the possibility "Ciceron" does not exist. This phonetic problem implies a consequent semantic deficiency that would indicate that Barbouillé has not been able to translate the Latin he has heard. In this case, Barbouillé's insufficiency is costly for "audi, quaeso" means "je vous écoute." Thus we are forced to conclude that Barbouillé is even unaware of when his "destinataire" is supposedly listening.

We can summarize the reasons for the failure of effective communication between Barbouillé and the doctor as founded on the confrontation between two completely different systems of language which remain unmodified and therefore without real contact. The doctor has betrayed a certain pretentiousness by his desire to redirect all linguistic stimuli to a consideration of his own qualities. This process rejects all attempts to understand the *meaning of the message transmitted* for a control rather of the discursive *form* and the *meaning of the words* of each message. Thus if we consider Benveniste's[30] description of the linguistic message:

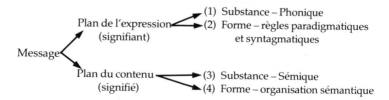

we see that this control is exercised at the levels of "forme du contenu" and "forme de l'expression" (4 et 2). In the first case, this manipulation destroys the linearity of the message and therefore all possibility of communication. For example, in the exchange:

> B: Vous êtes galant homme. . .
> D: Sais-tu d'où vient le mot de GALANT HOMME?

the relationship between the parts of the stimulus is destroyed in favor of a paradigmatic detour. The latter responds to an utterance as a linguistic sign to be analyzed in its form and not as a sign which derives its meaning from the syntactic and referential context in which it is used. Moreover, the doctor's control of the form (*de l'expression*) of the message he receives, as for example:

> B: Monsieur le docteur. . .
> D: Voilà qui est bien commencé. . .
> B: A la mienne volonté. . .

---

[30] Emile Benveniste, *Problèmes de linguistique générale* (Paris, 1966), pp. 119ff.

D: Voilà qui est bien. . .
B: J'enrage.
D: Otez-moi ce mot 'j'enrage'. . . (p. 15)

limits Barbouillé's choice of paradigmatic substitutions in the formation of syntagmatic units, and again modifies his language to the point where it loses all characteristics pertinent to its personal expression.

The word-play that we have been studying so far and the revelations that this study has shown for an understanding of Barbouillé's linguistic inadequacies prepare us to accept as reasonable the ultimate deception of the play. Purely by accident, Barbouillé finds himself in a position to prove his wife's misbehavior. Yet he misses his opportunity, abandoning his superior position inside his house to see if his wife has actually killed herself. She has not, of course, and enters behind Barbouillé's back, who is thus placed in the position of guilt. This manipulation, the only conscious one in the play, has been poorly prepared, however, for Barbouillé's wife has shown no particular talent in this area. It is possible, then, only because of Barbouillé's credulousness. The spectator, however, has observed Barbouillé's inability to determine the veracity or the import of an other's language and is consequently not surprised when Barbouillé fails again in this case. Thus, his final appeal to the audience is greeted with ridicule:

Je me donne au diable, si j'ai sorti de la maison, et demandez plutôt à ces Monsieurs qui sont là-bas dans le parterre; . . .Ah! que l'innocence est opprimée! (p. 19)

This desired interrogation of the spectator indicates the only place where any resolution is possible. Unfortunately, as will be the case for Harpagon, the spectator's superior perception will be of no use to Barbouillé. Moreover, every character has exhibited a warped perception of reality. Thus, this play's ultimate resolution lies solely with the spectator, who alone is capable of distinguishing truth from deception.

X.   Structures of Communication and the Comic in Farce

The comic structures of communication in farce can be summarized by indicating the inadequacies in the process of message transference which our four plays expose. The four part theory of communication:

$$(D_1) \text{ encoding } \rightarrow \text{ transmission } \rightarrow \text{ reception } \rightarrow \text{ decoding } (D_2)$$

indicates the general steps in this process. Theater, we have seen, adds the further dimension of the spectator, wherein the conversation between two characters becomes a second *message* to be evaluated. Thus each step of the message-transfer process which takes place on stage is actually double. We can diagram this situation as follows:

$$D_1 \text{ encodes m } \longrightarrow D_2 \text{ decodes m}$$

M

spectator decodes M and m

This M is comprised of the information gathered by the

spectator concerning the relative systems of language involved in the transference of m. Our first conclusion, then, is that farce often concerns the *difference in comprehension of m* between spectator and listener (D2). For example, although Barbouillé fails to decode correctly the doctor's ostensible refusal of payment, the spectator nevertheless understands it. The situation is similar for Sganarelle's encounter with the Egyptians: the spectator is the only correct decoder of the latter's language. This process extends to the decoding of objects as well, as we have seen in *Le Cocu imaginaire* and *Le Médecin volant*, where the same data are presented to character and spectator alike yet only the latter perceives them correctly. Farce prefers to deal with absolute contradictions in this area: either the character has understood *nothing* or has understood the complete *opposite* of the message he "receives." No nuances are offered, none are understood. The problem is revealed primarily by the inadequacy of the listener's response, an inadequacy demonstrated by his failure to decode poly-phonic or poly-semantic utterances or his inability to decode false discourse. Thus the criticism that farce is simplistic is mistaken; it is actually *basic*, since it concerns fundamental problems in referential perception and message comprehension.

Farce, however, is not limited to problems of decoding. As revealed in Sganarelle's attempted dissimulation in *Le Mariage forcé*, the farcic technique often exposes inadequacies of encoding as well. The possible problems in this area are two-fold: either a character betrays a certain arbitrariness in the expression of his desires or he betrays an abnormal comprehension of the concepts he attempts to demonstrate. In the first case, farce often demonstrates this arbitrariness by placing expression and meaning in direct opposition, for example, verbose pronouncements on the virtue of brevity, rather than in their normal relationship of mutual complementarity. In the second case, the "fourbe" presents explanations which are totally incongruous (bonnet ‹ bonum est) and often demonstrates this incongruity (Sganarelle's victory over Marphurius and his philosophy of total uncertainty). In both cases, however, it is necessary to assume a certain separation between the encoder and his own words. Not only does he disregard their meaning, but he often relinquishes all control over them. We have seen this in Pancrace's language, which is composed of substitutions of entire paradigms, or again with Sganarelle (*Le Mariage forcé*), who is unable to continue his dissimulation. Thus in the area of encoding as well, farce investigates the elementary point of contact between a speaker and his language.

Furthermore, farce is preponderantly concerned with the physical aspects of the process of communication itself, namely transmission and reception of messages. Of all the messages in the four farces we have studied, only about ten percent actually reach and affect a listener as they were intended. This is due to the violation of the elementary necessities of communication as defined by the phatic, metalinguistic, and referential functions of message-transference. In some cases, the listener was actually absent yet the speaker continued as if he were really talking to one; in other cases, the speaker created his own listener by limiting the form and content of what he would discuss. Often the speaker destroyed the linearity of the communicative process, either by interruption or nonsequitur, or reduced it to a completely self-directed process.

At this point, it is significant to note what areas farce is *not* concerned with. In most of the "conversations" we have observed, the topic of discussion was never even communicated; rather, the supposed listener, be it Pancrace or the doctor in *La Jalousie du Barbouillé*, denied transmission of any message by redirecting the discussion toward a justification of his personal qualities. There is, for this reason, no debate in farce, if by debate we understand the logical discussion of a topic shared by two characters. Piaget's[31] concept of ego-centric speech is pertinent to this type of situation; language between fools and pedants in farce is often accessory.

The main characteristic of such speech is the funda-mentally non-social, and hence, non-communicative nature of each of its three manifestations: Repetition, Monologue, and Collective Monologue. In Repetition, the child enjoys repeat-ing words for their own sake, without any external adaptation or audience. In Monologue, he uses words to accelerate his action or to accomplish an action that would otherwise be impossible.[32] In Collective Monologue, the child is merely thinking out loud about what he is doing; he experiences no desire to communicate any information to the others in whose presence he finds himself.

This study has demonstrated the similarity between the conversations farce presents and these childish conversations. The doctor's language in *La Jalousie du Barbouillé* is almost totally repetitious:

> Qu'est ceci? quel désordre! Quelle querelle! quelle grabuge! quel vacarme. . .Qu'y a-t-il, Monsieur? Qu'y a-t-il? Qu'y a-t-il? Ça, ça, voyons un peu s'il n'y a pas moyen de vous mettre d'accord, que je sois votre pacificateur, que j'apporte l'union chez vous. (p. 12)

as are Pancrace's pronouncements on brevity. However, in two of the farces we have studied, there has been at least one character who turned all conversation with him into Collective Monologue: Pancrace with Sganarelle in *Le Mariage forcé*, and the doctor with Barbouillé in *La Jalousie du Barbouillé*. The result of all this abnormal language (between adults) is that the discussion never reaches the level of genuine argument. Nowhere is the word "because" to be found in the speech of

---

[31] Piaget, pp. 25 passim.

[32] For an excellent example of this, see Sganarelle's monologue in *Le Cocu imaginaire* (pp. 239–241).

Barbouillé, Gorgibus, or Sganarelle. Hence, there are no deductive or inductive arguments and consequently, no desire to convince; rather each seeks to overwhelm the other by the force of his presentation.

This final observation brings us to the ultimate problematic of language posed in farce: the inability of all characters (except the successful manipulators) to agree on, and therefore discuss, the consequences of one particular idea or behavior. Farce, it seems, is concerned with the inability to *denote* adequately the actions or ideas observed. Hence, farce's apparent unconcern for the possible misinterpretations of one and the same idea agreed upon by all—there is no such universally agreed upon idea.

Thus, just as it can be said that farce possesses aesthetic principles which determine it as a specific literary genre, it can also be concluded that the attention to language in farce is of a particular nature. This attention is simple only in appearance, since the farceur actually questions the prerequisites for any communication. In this sense, Molière's farces are more evidently universal in effect, albeit less rich, than plays such as *Tartuffe* or *Le Misanthrope*.

XI.   Farce and Molière's Moral of Language

It has been observed earlier that the dramatization of language's use and misuse, and the consequent ridiculing of certain types of linguistic behavior, necesarily implied a judgment of the "correct" purposes and inherent limitations of language itself according to the dramatist. This was an especially pertinent observation for comedy, a genre which is, if not corrective, at least normative in purpose. In Molière, language not only transcoded eccentric predispositions or systems; more importantly, it demonstrated how these predispositions were rooted in ridiculous communicative behavior, thus evoking laughter in the spectator and inviting him to elaborate the dramatist's implicit moral of language. Having summarized the structures of this comic communicative behavior in four farces, it would now be appropriate to make explicit the particular moral of language each play presents.

In *La Jalousie du Barbouillé*, the principal communicative behavior of the play, Barbouillé's attempt to seek advice from a "docteur" and the attempt by all characters to explain the cause of their dispute to the latter, resulted in no actual message-transference. In the first case, the doctor succeeded in re-directing his interlocutor's words to an area within which he could flaunt his own "knowledge"; in the second case, this same doctor exasperated all concerned by his refusal to hear any message not formulated according to his notion of appropriateness. Barbouillé's inability to affect the doctor was not gratuitous, however, since it was directly related to his inability to decode reality correctly, as his wife's final deception indicated. By frustrating communication at every turn, and by relating this frustration to complementarily inadequate speech systems, Molière demonstrated that communication between interlocutors who are totally preoccupied with themselves is impossible. Self-interest alone, therefore, cannot effect communication; the desired respondent must in some way be convinced to make this interest his own, at least initially. Where this is not achieved, only the non-solution of this case, consistent with the total failure to communicate, is possible.

In *Sganarelle ou le Cocu imaginaire*, Molière examined the effects on communication when interlocutors are only too ready to decode reality or to accept the messages transmitted by another. In this curious play where no reflective manipulation of language took place, it was seen how speech could serve to confirm and propagate errors in the perception of reality and in the decoding of words where there exists a climate of inherent suspiciousness. For the couple Sganarelle-wife, Molière demonstrated the possibility of language to appear logical and illogical at the same time; divorced from referential reality, any speech becomes merely incidental, and its truth or falsity impossible to ascertain. For the couple Célie-Lélie, Molière presented the convincing nature of even speech based on false perception where the desire to believe refused all opposing evidence. By juxtaposing the misperception of physical reality and the miscomprehension of speech, Molière thus demonstrated the similarity between these two problems:

the ultimate truth value of language lies not with the speaker but rather with observable facts.

In these two farces, therefore, Molière examined two fundamental necessities for effective communication: adaptation of language to the desired listener and correct perception of referential reality. In the first case, the spectator's comic judgment was directed against all characters, but especially against the doctor, whose preoccupation with self doomed all messages to non-transmission. The transparency of this obstacle to communication made all participants seem ridiculous: Barbouillé and the others since they could not overcome this obstacle and the doctor since he seemed unaware of his own interference. In the second case, the spectator's judgment was similarly directed against all characters since their mutual suspicions precluded any investigation of the misperception upon which all their speech was based. In both cases, the problems of language were not only fundamental but also immediately apparent. Molière's investigation will go much further than this, however, as for example in the series of plays consisting of *Le Médecin volant, Le Médecin malgré lui,* and *Les Fourberies de Scapin,* where he presents the conscious use of language to misrepresent reality. In these plays, four important, interdependent methods of this misrepresentation are examined and explained: language as disguise ("se faire paraître"), as persuasion ("faire croire"), as complement or substitute for action ("faire faire"), and as self-deception ("se faire croire").

Sganarelle's deception of Gorgibus in *Le Médecin volant* presented a complete yet rather schematic dramatization of language's persuasive power. This deception principally involved the creation of disguise through speech (medical jargon) and objects (change of dress). Language here merely supported referential observation, however, and Sganarelle's success was clearly based on the incredible stupidity of Gorgibus, whose desire to believe blinded him to the inherent illogicality of the "fourbe's" speech. Only the *appearance* of a doctoral identity was necessary, therefore, since Gorgibus believed in an inherent identification between speech and being. Molière here did not examine the power of the language of someone who *is* a doctor, as he would in *Le Malade imaginaire*, but rather the power of language to support an appearance of "doctorness." There is an a priori limit to the effectiveness of such language, however, as evidenced by the facility with which the spectator saw through Sganarelle's speech: where the jargon used is incorrectly formulated, the true source of any power lies in the believability of the role created, not the language itself. It is for this reason that Sganarelle can be exposed even by Gorgibus since deception which depends on the manipulation of reality is destined ultimately to be confronted by this reality and thus uncovered. Language, therefore, has its limits; it cannot create physical reality.

In *Le Mariage forcé*, Molière underlined the power of language to deceive its own speaker. In this case, the Sganarelle involved in self-deception revealed the reason for his dissimulation in the very act of attempting to manipulate his listener. By revealing Sganarelle's abnormal conception of communication as merely a search for affirmation of what was already believed, Molière gave an important new meaning to gratuitous interruption such as the doctor's in *La Jalousie*. Pancrace's and Marphurius' linguistic systems seemed particularly appropriate obstacles for a character for whom a listener was superfluous and who feigned doubt where none existed. Moreover, Molière demonstrated the dangers of presenting oneself under a self-deceiving disguise: language which dissimulates, whether effectively or ineffectively, is nevertheless persuasive, since it depends on what its listener chooses to believe. Most important, however, was Molière's investigation of the optimistic and skeptical theories of language. Both are inadequate, since the first fails to account for the modifications of speech necessitated by changing respondents and the second disregards the objective truth value of physical reality. "Correct" language, therefore, would include speech which is flexible, that is, not limited to some abstract notion of appropriateness to thought, and which is at all times directly related to its referent.

Part Three:

NEW DIRECTIONS FOR MOLIÈRE SCHOLARSHIP

XII. Methodological Results of This Study

We stated at the outset of this study that we had encountered significant gaps in the critical literature bearing on
Molière which specifically involved the nature and function of
language within his dramatic corpus. Although Molière critics
had dealt with language in one form or another, none seemed
to attribute to this area the importance we felt it deserved. Our
analysis of four farces has demonstrated, however, that attention to Molière's language in its communicative manifestations
on stage can be particularly fruitful in the understanding of
these plays' internal coherence. Although results such as these
were an important part of our purpose, we were not primarily
interested in proposing radical re-interpretations. We sought
instead to examine language in these farces not solely as a
vehicle of their author's positions, but more importantly as a
distinct area of interest on his part, in order to reach some
tentative conclusions on Molière's moral of language use.
Equally important as this study of Molière's language on its
own terms was our interest in developing an appropriate
linguistic methodology which would give adequate expression to the primacy of language within the comic phenome-

non. Before concluding with several further applications of this methodology, we must therefore first indicate its value by examining how it enables us to understand more clearly three important problem areas: (a) the relationship of language to the comic; (b) the role of comic verbal exchange in Molière; (c) the implicit content of Molière's moral of language as revealed by the interplay of these verbal exchanges within the context of comedy.

In developing a methodology, we stated our fundamental agreement with the insights of Freud, Bergson, and Mauron on the nature of the comic phenomenon. While differing perhaps in emphasis and purpose, these three theorists agreed on several necessary conditions for the comic reaction: the comic required a comparison between character and spectator which would result in an affective distance between them and make possible a feeling of superiority in the latter. By seeking the terms of this comparison in the observation of linguistic behavior, we immediately profited from the nature of language itself. As both social and individual, language is inherently comparative, for it is at once norm and usage, system and personal appropriation of system. Thus, any character involved in its use automatically revealed the difference between his understanding of the fundamental units of his language and the spectator's understanding, and at the same time assured the correct comprehension of this difference. This comparison between character and spectator on the level of codal competence was perhaps the most fundamental source of the comic, for it involved the basic contact between a speaker and the meaning of his own words.

Although this comparison between specifically codal competencies seems to play a lesser role in the more developed plays, the observation of language as an important type of action did facilitate the determination of several more important comparisons between characters and between spectator and character. In the first place, whether accompanied by or substituted for action, the linguistic behavior of any character was immediately possible to judge as adequate or inadequate, for the spectator could always decode what was meant and compare the result with the response engendered on stage. Thus in concentrating specifically on the language of deception, for example, we showed how the spectator could remain superior to both deceiver and deceived, for the absurdity of the "fourbe's" jargon was immediately transparent, and the dupe's acceptance of it was an indication of its effectiveness despite this evident inadequacy.

Yet language's ultimate importance for the comic goes beyond such categories of comparison as competence and adequacy. As the articulated evidence of its speaker's perception of surrounding reality, language does more than simply express desire; at this more profound level, its use reveals the results of a speaker's attempt to order and give meaning to the stimuli with which he is presented, and most importantly *in a code accessible to all*. Explicitly or implicitly, consciously or unconsciously, then, language encodes the moral and psychological priorities of its user, and reveals both the principles and the results of their structuring. If the comic judgment is inherently a normative one, then the observation of language is one of its more important comparative aspects, since the act of speech reveals the very structure of the being that is judged. Any theory of the comic, therefore, must afford a position of priority to the comic revealed by the use of language, for this use appears to be the point of convergence for the comic of action, of words, and of character.[1]

By emphasizing the specific use of language in communication, we demonstrated that beneath the veneer of its

---

[1] In our analysis, which begins with the examination of speech, linguistic inadequacy implies perceptual inadequacy. The situation is clearly the reverse from any speaker's point of view, since for him perception precedes its expression in language.

traditional comic situations, even Molière's farces dealt profoundly with problems of language. This deeper level of inquiry does not, and should not, deny the plays any sociological, philosophical or psychological importance, but rather, must draw upon and profit from their implications in order to sharpen the presentation of the particular communicative problem in question. Intra- and extra-marital difficulties, father versus son confrontation, philosophical and medical satire, pure deception even, often serve as *cadres* in Molière's theater for the more specifically linguistic and discursive questions of denotation, conceptualization, the implicit in language, the creation and transmission of fiction in the guise of truth. These questions are of particular interest, for the characters involved in such situations all reveal through their linguistic acts a certain position vis-à-vis language and the act of communication itself, a position which, when confronted by or used against that of another, defines and presents to the spectator a discursive situation. This situation, analyzable in its stimulus-response patterns, invites the spectator to bring his normative judgment to bear on its interlocutors, *and hence on their positions*. Ambiguous encoding, inadequate transmission, imperfect decoding, whether conscious or not, constitute the message (M) received by the spectator which enables him to *understand and evaluate* the psychology of the speakers and the nature of their inter-relationships. Since this message is both meaning and comparison, it guarantees intellectual comprehension and affective distance at the same time.

XIII.   A New Look at Three-
and Five-Act Comedy

We chose to examine structures of communication in four of Molière's farces on both methodological and formal grounds. It seemed appropriate to begin the development of a linguistic method where language use was most basic and with a genre whose language was mistakenly considered of secondary importance. The ultimate validity of our approach, however, lies in its applicability to other plays of different form and content. Before concluding with several observations on Molière's general philosophy of language, we would therefore propose to analyze briefly five additional plays by demonstrating how our methodology can reveal their linguistic preoccupations.

From a communicative perspective, the most evident difference between Molière's farces and his more lengthy plays is the increase in the number of messages effectively transmitted. This difference indicates that the latter emphasize the *nature* of encoding and decoding, rather than the physical problems of communication. Thus, for example, the fourbe's language does not simply confuse or deceive, but rather encodes two messages simultaneously which divert the attention of the dupe and support the deception of the lovers. In *Le Médecin malgré lui*, Sganarelle uses his "medical" discourse to communicate the necessary course of action to the suitor and to baffle the opposing father at the same time:

> Sg: . . .un remède. . .qui est une prise
>   de fuite purgative. . .avec deux
>   drachmes de matrimonium en pilules.
> G: Quelles drogues, Monsieur, sont celles
>   que vous venez de dire? (pp. 44–45)

In *L'Ecole des maris*, Valère's and Isabelle's deceptive speech operates in the same manner; each succeeds in encoding two messages, one for the other partner, which develops their relationship, and one for Sganarelle, which seems to confirm his victory:

> Sg: Elle [Isabelle] vient de m'en faire entière
>   confidence;
>   Et de plus m'a chargé de vous [Valère] donner avis
>   Que depuis que par vous tous ses pas sont suivis,
>   Son coeur, qu'avec excès votre poursuite outrage,
>   N'a que trop de vos yeux entendu le langage,
>   Que vos secrets désirs lui sont assez connus,
>   Et que c'est vous donner des soucis superflus,
>   De vouloir d'avantage expliquer une flamme
>   Qui choque l'amitié que me garde son âme.

In *Les Fourberies de Scapin*, the two messages are encoded for the spectator; by lying to Argante and Géronte, and having them believe him, Scapin reveals their credulousness and true avaricious nature at the same time.

The problems of decoding are also more developed in three-act comedy. While those deceived still exhibit the same weaknesses which make their deception possible, greed and self-sufficiency, the presentation of these weaknesses is different. Farce tends to present them in an a priori fashion; this is the way a character acts because this is what he is. In the plays we have just mentioned, however, the decoder is given the opportunity to demonstrate his weaknesses to characters and spectator alike. Thus, in *Le Médecin malgré lui*, Géronte reveals the isolation he has imposed on his daughter at the same time as she is escaping him. In *Les Fourberies de Scapin*, all we know of Argante's and Géronte's nature is what Scapin forces them to betray by his deceptions. In *L'Ecole des maris*, Sganarelle reveals himself throughout the entire first act. The result of this emphasis on the nature of the decoder is to justify the methods by which he is deceived. Molière thus not only seeks to assure the decoder's belief in the encoder's deceptive message, but to assure that this belief is credible for the spectator as well. Thus a tighter relationship between speech structures and reasons for deception is established, giving a feeling of rigorous demonstration to the plays. The use of language in communicative situations, therefore, not only *reveals* character inadequacies, but *demonstrates* by its very form the nature and extent of these inadequacies; in speaking, the comic character not only unwittingly relates his preoccupations, but acts them out as well by demonstrating their detrimental effect on his social behavior.

Le Médecin malgré lui, unlike *Le Médecin volant*, does not involve a manipulation by objects. Sganarelle's deception of Géronte in this case is based on the latter's belief in his "doctorness," yet this role needs only the words of others (Martine ⟶ Valère ⟶ Lucas ⟶ Géronte) for its creation. This difference is crucial, however, since only Martine possesses the knowledge necessary to expose Sganarelle's lexically correct medical language. Since he is aware only of the results of his power and not its source, Sganarelle actually comes to believe in his role. In this particular play, therefore, Molière seems primarily interested in demonstrating the effects of language's persuasive power on both "fourbe" and "fou" alike. In Sganarelle's original conflict with Martine, however, Molière demonstrates how physical force could be both an asset and a liability for discursive power. By presenting Sganarelle as an effective manipulator of language who nevertheless resorts to force where unnecessary, the dramatist prepares the spectator for this character's later defeat by two discursively ineffective yet forcefully superior manipulators. In the speech of Martine, he demonstrates the power of language to create truth *from a distance* and defend its creation by exploiting its listener's desire to believe.

Les Fourberies de Scapin presents several important modifications in the sources of language's persuasive power. No manipulation by objects here, nor recourse to physical force; Scapin's language depends exclusively on his ability to exploit his dupes' inherent obsessions. This use of language as pure fabrication relying neither on the disguising of its speaker nor on an unknown jargon for its acceptance as truth represents the culmination of manipulatory speech in Molière. Persuasion in this play joins credulity to obsession in a way which demonstrates this obsession as the source of gullibility and the justification for deception. In this sense, Molière portrays the intimate connection between character eccentricity and decoding priorities, demonstrating that the exploitation of the latter can also bring about the revelation of the former.

Although Scapin is aware throughout that his persuasive power lies in the exploitation of obsession, in his final attempt, he deceives himself into believing that any type of deception is possible. Obsessed himself with the desire for vengeance, he attempts a manipulation of objective reality similar to Sganarelle's in *Le Médecin volant*; in this case, however, the "fourbe" seeks to create, not atomize, physical objects by language. Molière's message here is evident: to the degree that Scapin considers his power to depend primarily on his own words, *and not also on their interpretation by a listener*, he allows his own self-deception. If language must be modified in transmission in order to be communicative, then, it must also be modified by a listener in order to permit the persuasiveness of its fabrications.

In *L'Ecole des maris*, this notion of self-deception is amplified to include the first system of principles in Molière's theater. The demonstration in this play is two-fold: not only are Sganarelle's precepts revealed as ridiculous, but their presentation as a logical, theoretical system is shown to be a simple mask for their basis in egocentric fear and defensive self-justification. Molière demonstrates the extent of Sganarelle's blindness by making of him the unwitting go-between for the effective communicators, Valère and Isabelle. Thus the structures which would refuse communication become the very reason communication is effected; Valère and Isabelle exploit Sganarelle exactly where he believes his strength to lie.

Le Bourgeois Gentilhomme differs significantly from the plays we just summarized; Monsieur Jourdain not only presents all the characteristics of the typical comic fool—self-deception, credulity, obsession—but also represents a specific social class. Thus Molière's investigation of language goes beyond the area of pure linguistic deception to portray the fundamental relationship between communicative structures and social stratification. Jourdain's language demonstrates the ineffectiveness of bourgeois concepts for the appropriation of the aristocratic world. This intrinsic ineffectiveness, however, applies on a more profound level to the appropriation of any knowledge; Jourdain's preoccupation with the immediately perceptible aspects of reality, and his satisfaction with the "knowledge" this perception affords him, reveals Molière's interest in the primal relationship between man and reality. Within Molière's moral of language, then, this play becomes much more than a simple demonstration of bourgeois inferiority: *Le Bourgeois Gentilhomme* attests to the fact that if reality is more than nomenclature, the language which would express and understand it must be more than metalinguistic.

The problems of language presented in *George Dandin* are both social and individual. In this play, Molière demonstrates how even reflection, as concretized in monologue, can be self-deceiving and ineffective although it may be based on a true perception of reality. Although it can be shown that Dandin's ostensibly justifiable formulations are in fact mere masks for more profound personal inadequacies and therefore that his deception by Angélique is deserved, the ultimate problem of inherent aristocratic power over truth gives this play a "dramatic" tone. Unlike the dupes who precede him, Dandin's "truth" is also the spectator's; he is at all times correct insofar as the facts of his situation are concerned. That Clitandre can deny these facts by the simple recourse to his social position is serious, therefore, since such denial represents an arbitrary definition of truth as the word of a noble. This struggle of the individual against the tyranny of social language will find its ultimate echo in Alceste.

In general, therefore, Molière's theater reveals the problematic nature of language in its communicative function. The optimistic theory that supposes a strict correspondence between thought and speech is inadequate for two reasons: first, speech often unconsciously affirms *more* or *less* than the speaker's intentions, thus revealing that it is not a simple series of external signs expressing an internal reality; secondly, speech can be used designedly to deceive, thus indicating that an intermediate context, personal desire, can purposely obscure the relationship between words and meaning. The skeptic's position that no language can adequately express thought or reality is equally untenable; despite all difficulties, speech can succeed in expressing intention and in accounting for observable facts. As a product of his age, Molière would certainly have preferred to believe in the optimist's exact equivalence of rational thought and speech, and in man's ability to uncover the truth behind inherently deceptive appearances. And yet, as a dramatist dedicated to unmasking the weaknesses of man, he could not ignore the fact that this theory was inadequate, that there existed a level of truth which could be determined only by attention to appearances. His dramatic corpus is thus curiously paradoxical: whereas its entire movement is toward revealing the unfaithful nature of speech to encode or decode thought, its philosophical presupposition is that *his* speech can be encoded clearly and decoded unambiguously by his audience. No one more than the author of *Tartuffe* realized the difficulty of this task; as a classical dramatist, however, he would have no other choice than to place his faith in the power of language to express his thought. In the last analysis, Molière found himself in an impossible position: he could operate with neither a perfect language nor a problematic one. His subject was the falsity of speech supposedly rational; in order to alert his spectators to it, his own speech could leave no doubt as to its meaning. And yet, this same speech remained anchored in the problematic world of appearances which it sought to unmask. In short, Molière sought to demonstrate the problematic nature of language by means of a language which would be nonproblematic, a state it could not fully attain.

XIV: Conclusion

Linguistic analysis of farce has revealed that this genre questions the nature of communicative language in its fundamental aspects. In this sense, the comic which is derived from farcic situations is almost universal: gratuitous interruption, nonsequitur, verbose pronouncements on brevity, misused logic and codal incompetence can be appreciated in much the same way by the classical and modern spectator. The linguistic comedy in Molière's farces is thus an important clue to their continued appreciation. More importantly, however, to the degree that attention to language in all its forms is a unifying theme of Molière's theater, plays whose subjects might be considered less topical in the twentieth century acquire other contemporary meanings. *Tartuffe* certainly questions the nature of religion under Louis XIV; *Le Misanthrope* paints a clear picture of "la cour"; *Le Malade imaginaire* reveals much about 17th century medicine. In linguistic terms, however, Tartuffe is more than a classical "faux dévot"; he is a master of linguistic disguise hiding behind a discourse whose terms are sacrosanct despite their inherent ambiguity. Similarly, Alceste's sincerity, while certainly comic to the nobles of his audience, is perhaps less so in an era when the problematicity of language is so evident. Finally, while we may have gone beyond the 17th century's questions of medical experimentation and the circulation of the blood, we have not yet learned to decode the difference between medical technology and medical guesswork. In this sense, therefore, religion, class, and medicine can be considered as frameworks for what is truly modern about Molière—the use and abuse of language.

Molière was not a philosopher or linguist in the scientific sense of these terms, and it has not been our intention to portray him as such. Yet as a comic dramatist, he could not ignore the ridiculous in either its practical or theoretical form. The misuse of language was the most direct observation he could make in order to ridicule the bourgeois and the noble, the dévot, philosopher, or doctor. Implicitly, however, he could not avoid reaching the theoretical presuppositions of their behavior as well. However unclear Molière's relationship to Gassendi, Descartes, or Port-Royal might be, it is probable that their linguistic philosophies had some effect on his own thinking. Pancrace's speech on the relationship between thought and language is remarkably similar to Arnauld's treatment of the same subject in *La Grammaire générale et raisonnée de Port-Royal*; Marphurius is a classical skeptical thinker. Similarities such as these deserve a much more extensive analysis, for they seem particularly striking and could lead to a clearer statement of Molière's position vis-à-vis actual 17th century linguistic thought.

Ultimately, a linguistic approach to the problem of genre definition can be quite revealing. Just as each communicative act is in a sense a re-definition of speech itself, each act of literary expression re-defines literature. By creating literature from the spoken word, Molière attempted both, questioning language's inherent capabilities and limitations as he created classical comedy as we know it. In analyzing his farces in this complementary way, as language and literary investigation of language, we have tried to demonstrate the relationship between form and content for Molière. This relationship finds its clearest expression in the ultimate problematicity of the playwright's task: to formalize his message with a far less than perfect medium. Linguistic attention to form, therefore, is a particularly appropriate methodology, for it can structure the literary message on this message's own terms.

Bibliography

Barthes, Roland. *Les Eléments de sémiologie*. Paris: Editions du Seuil, 1964.
Benveniste, Emile. *Problèmes de linguistique générale*. Paris: Gallimard, 1966
Bergson, Henri. *Le Rire: Essai sur la signification du comique*. 1901; rpt. Paris: Presses Universitaries de France, 1972.
Bowen, Barbara. *Les Caractéristiques essentielles de la farce française et leur survivance dans les années 1550–1620*. Urbana: University of Illinois Press, 1964.
Bray, René. *Molière, homme de théâtre*. Paris: Mercure de France, 1954.
Dubois, Jacques, et al. *Rhétorique générale*. Paris: Larousse, 1970.
Ducrot, Oswald. *Dire et ne pas dire*. Paris: Hermann, 1972.
Freud, Sigmund. *Jokes and Their Relation to the Unconscious*. 1905; rpt. New York: W.W. Norton and Co., 1963.
Garapon, Robert. *La Fantaisie verbale et le comique dans le théâtre français*. Paris: Colin, 1957.
Greimas, A.J. *Sémantique structurale*. Paris: Larousse, 1966.
Guicharnaud, Jacques. *Molière: Une Aventure théâtrale*. Paris: Gallimard, 1963.
Hubert, Judd. *Molière and the Comedy of Intellect*. Los Angeles: University of California Press, 1962.
Jakobson, Roman. *Essais de linguistique générale*. Paris: Editions de Minuit, 1963.
Lanson, Gustave. "Molière and Farce." In *Comedy: Meaning and Form*. Ed. Robert Corrigan. Scranton: Chandler Publishing Co., 1965, pp. 378–396.
Larthomas, Pierre. *Le Langage dramatique*. Paris: Colin, 1972.
Le Guern, Michel. *Sémantique de la métaphore et de la métonymie*. Paris: Larousse, 1973.
Lyons, John, ed. *New Horizons in Linguistics*. Great Britain: Penguin Books, 1970.
Martinet, André. *Eléments de linguistique générale*. 2nd ed. Paris: Colin, 1967.
Mauron, Charles. *Psychocritique du genre comique*. Paris: Corti, 1964.

Merleau-Ponty, Maurice. *Signes*. Paris: Gallimard, 1960.

Miller, George. *Langage et Communication*. Paris: Presses Universitaires de France, 1956.

Moore, Will. *Molière: A New Criticism*. 1949; rpt. New York: Doubleday and Co., 1962.

Molière. *Oeuvres complètes*. Robert Jouanny, ed. 2 vols. Paris: Garnier Frères, 1962.

Piaget, Jean. *The Language and Thought of the Child*. Trans. Marjorie Gabain. New York: The World Publishing Co., 1971.

Plato. "Cratyle." In *The Collected Dialogues*. Edith Hamilton, ed. New York: Pantheon Books, 1961.

De Saussure, Ferdinand. *Cours de linguistique générale*. Tulio de Mauro, ed. Paris: Payot, 1972.

Scherer, Jacques. *La Dramaturgie classique en France*. Paris: Nizet, 1970.

Index

143

144

stuòia humanitatis

PUBLISHED VOLUMES

Louis Marcello La Favia, *Benvenuto Rambaldi da Imola: Dantista*. xii–188 pp. US $9.25.

John O'Connor, *Balzac's Soluble Fish*. xii–252 pp. US $14.25.

Carlos García, *La desordenada codicia*, edición crítica de Giulio Massano. xii–220 pp. US $11.50.

Everett W. Hesse, *Interpretando la Comedia*. xii–184 pp. US $10.00.

Lewis Kamm, *The Object in Zola's* Rougon-Macquart. xii–160 pp. US $9.25.

Ann Bugliani, *Women and the Feminine Principle in the Works of Paul Claudel*. xii–144 pp. US $9.25.

Charlotte Frankel Gerrard, *Montherlant and Suicide*. xvi–72 pp. US $5.00.

The Two Hesperias. Literary Studies in Honor of Joseph G. Fucilla. Edited by Americo Bugliani. xx–372 pp. US $30.00.

Jean J. Smoot, *A Comparison of Plays by John M. Synge and Federico García Lorca: The Poets and Time*. xiii–220 pp. US $13.00.

Laclos. Critical Approaches to Les Liaisons dangereuses. Ed. Lloyd R. Free. xii–300 pp. US $17.00.

145

Julia Conaway Bondanella, *Petrarch's Visions and their Renaissance Analogues*. xii–120 pp. US $7.00.

Vincenzo Tripodi, *Studi su Foscolo e Stern*. xii–216 pp. US $13.00.

Genaro J. Pérez, *Formalist Elements in the Novels of Juan Goytisolo*. xii–216 pp. US $12.50.

Sara Maria Adler, *Calvino: The Writer as Fablemaker*. xviii–164 pp. US $11.50.

Lope de Vega, *El amor enamorado*, critical edition of John B. Wooldridge, Jr. xvi–236 pp. US $13.00.

Nancy Dersofi, *Arcadia and the Stage: A Study of the Theater of Angelo Beolco* (called *Ruzante*). xii–180 pp. US $10.00

John A. Frey, *The Aesthetics of the* Rougon-Macquart. xvi–356 pp. US $20.00.

Chester W. Obuchowski, *Mars on Trial: War as Seen by French Writers of the Twentieth Century*. xiv–320 pp. US $20.00.

Jeremy T. Medina, *Spanish Realism: Theory and Practice of a Concept in the Nineteenth Century*. xviii–374 pp. US $17.50.

Mauda Bregoli-Russo, *Boiardo Lirico*. viii–204 pp. US $11.00.

Robert H. Miller, ed. *Sir John Harington: A Supplie or Addicion to the Catalogue of Bishops to the Yeare 1608*. xii–214 pp. US $13.50.

Nicolás E. Álvarez, *La obra literaria de Jorge Mañach*. vii–279 pp. US $13.00.

Mario Aste, *La narrativa di Luigi Pirandello: Dalle novelle al romanzo Uno, Nessuno, e Centomila*. xvi–200 pp. US $11.00.

Mechthild Cranston, *Orion Resurgent: René Char, Poet of Presence*. xxiv–376 pp. U.S. $22.50.

Frank A. Domínguez, *The Medieval Argonautica*. viii–122 pp. US $8.50.

EVERETT HESSE, *New Perspectives on Comedia Criticism.* xix–174 pp. US $14.00.

ANTHONY A. CICCONE, *The Comedy of Language: Four Farces by Molière.* xii–144 $12.50.

ANTONIO PLANELLS, *Cortázar: Metafísica y erotismo.* xvi–220 pp. US $10.00.

MARY LEE BRETZ, *La evolución novelística de Pío Baroja.* vii–470 pp. US $22.50.

Romance Literary Studies: Homage to Harvey L. Johnson, ed. Marie A. Wellington and Martha O'Nan. xxxvii–185 pp. US $15.00.

FORTHCOMING PUBLICATIONS

El cancionero del Bachiller Jhoan López, edición crítica de Rosalind Gabin.

Studies in Honor of Gerald E. Wade, edited by Sylvia Bowman, Bruno M. Damiani, Janet W. Díaz, E. Michael Gerli, Everett Hesse, John E. Keller, Luis Leal and Russell Sebold.

HELMUT HATZFELD, *Essais sur la littérature flamboyante.*

JOSEPH BARBARINO, *The Latin Intervocalic Stops: A Quantitative and Comparative Study.*

NANCY D'ANTUONO, *Boccaccio's novelle in Lope's theatre.*

Novelistas femeninas de la postguerra española, ed. Janet W. Díaz.

La Discontenta and La Pythia, edition with introduction and notes by Nicholas A. De Mara.

PERO LÓPEZ DE AYALA, *Crónica del Rey Don Pedro I,* edición crítica de Heanon y Constance Wilkins.

ALBERT H. LE MAY, *The Experimental Verse Theater of Valle-Inclán.*

MARIA ELISA CIAVARELLI, *La fuerza de la sangre en la literatura del Siglo de Oro.*

DENNIS M. KRATZ, *Mocking Epic.*

CALDERÓN DE LA BARCA, *The Prodigal Magician,* translated and edited by Bruce W. Wardropper.

GEORGE E. McSPADDEN, *Don Quixote and the Spanish Prologues,* volume I.

LOIS ANN RUSSELL, *Robert Challe: A Utopian Voice in the Early Enlightenment.*

CRAIG WALLACE BARROW, *Montage in James Joyce's* ULYSSES.